OHIO TEST PREP

Practice Test Book

Mathematics

Grade 5

ISBN 978-1731373724

TEST MASTER PRESS

www.testmasterpress.com

CONTENTS

INTRODUCTION
For Parents, Teachers, and Tutors

About Ohio's Mathematics Assessments

Students take Ohio's State Test for Mathematics each year. The test is made up of around 50 questions that assess all the skills in Ohio's Learning Standards. The questions have a range of formats including multiple-choice, technology-enhanced, short answer, as well as questions that require students to explain a concept or justify an answer. This book will develop all the mathematics skills that students need, while giving students ongoing practice answering all types of test questions.

About Ohio's Mathematics Standards

Student learning in Ohio is based on the skills described in Ohio's Learning Standards. In 2017, Ohio's Learning Standards for Mathematics were revised. Beginning in the 2018-2019 school year, the state tests will assess these revised standards. Just like the real state tests, the questions in this book assess whether students have the knowledge and skills described in the revised standards.

Developing Mathematics Skills

Ohio's Learning Standards require students to have a thorough and in-depth understanding of mathematics skills, as well as the ability to apply the skills to solve problems. To ensure that students have the abilities needed, the practice sets contain rigorous questions that require students to explain concepts, apply skills, complete tasks, or describe how a problem was solved. These advanced questions will ensure that students gain an in-depth understanding of the skills. This will also help students apply the skills to solve a wide range of problems when completing the state tests.

Taking the Tests

The first four practice sets introduce students to the assessments with 10 questions. The first two sets contain only multiple-choice questions, while the second two sets contain a range of question types. These short tests will allow students to become familiar with assessment questions before moving on to longer tests. These shorter tests may also be used as guided instruction before allowing students to complete the assessments on their own.

The remaining practice sets each have 20 questions with a wide range of question formats. By completing the practice sets, students will have ongoing practice with assessment items, develop the math skills they need, gain experience with all types of test questions, and be fully prepared for Ohio's Mathematics assessments.

Mathematics

Grade 5

Practice Set 1

Instructions

Read each question carefully. For each multiple-choice question, fill in the circle for the correct answer.

This test should take 30 minutes to complete.

1   The Greenway Softball Club made $2,160 by holding a carwash. The softball club wants to divide the money evenly between the 12 teams in the club. How much will each team receive?

    Ⓐ $120

    Ⓑ $140

    Ⓒ $160

    Ⓓ $180

2   The shaded parts of the model represent a fraction.

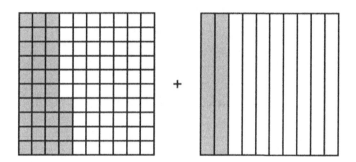

What is the sum of the fractions?

    Ⓐ $\dfrac{36}{100}$

    Ⓑ $\dfrac{54}{100}$

    Ⓒ $\dfrac{36}{110}$

    Ⓓ $\dfrac{54}{110}$

3   Winona has 48 stamps. She has 6 times as many stamps as Catherine. How many stamps does Catherine have?

Ⓐ   8

Ⓑ   9

Ⓒ   42

Ⓓ   288

4   William surveyed students on how long it took them to travel to school each morning. The table shows the results.

Time	Number of Students
0 to 10 minutes	22
11 to 30 minutes	36
31 to 60 minutes	14
Over 60 minutes	3

Which type of graph would William be best to use to summarize the survey results?

Ⓐ   Bar graph

Ⓑ   Scatterplot

Ⓒ   Line graph

Ⓓ   Stem-and-leaf plot

5   What is the value of $\frac{9}{12} - \frac{3}{12}$?

   Ⓐ $\frac{1}{12}$

   Ⓑ $\frac{3}{12}$

   Ⓒ $\frac{5}{12}$

   Ⓓ $\frac{6}{12}$

6   There are 365 days in a year and 24 hours in a day. How many hours are there in a year?

   Ⓐ   8,540

   Ⓑ   8,560

   Ⓒ   8,740

   Ⓓ   8,760

7   Which shape always has two pairs of congruent sides?

   Ⓐ   square

   Ⓑ   rectangle

   Ⓒ   rhombus

   Ⓓ   trapezoid

8   Which statement describes the value of the expression below?

$$40 \times \frac{1}{8}$$

   Ⓐ   The value is greater than 40.

   Ⓑ   The value is less than 40.

   Ⓒ   The value is equal to 40.

   Ⓓ   The value is between 0 and 1.

9   Which term describes the triangle below?

   Ⓐ   Isosceles

   Ⓑ   Scalene

   Ⓒ   Equilateral

   Ⓓ   Right

10   A baby elephant was born at a zoo. The elephant weighed 184 pounds. What is the weight, in ounces, of the elephant?

Ⓐ   1,840 ounces

Ⓑ   2,208 ounces

Ⓒ   2,944 ounces

Ⓓ   3,312 ounces

END OF PRACTICE SET

Mathematics

Grade 5

Practice Set 2

Instructions

Read each question carefully. For each multiple-choice question, fill in the circle for the correct answer.

This test should take 30 minutes to complete.

1   Which expression can represent 4 less than the quotient of 192 and 3?

   Ⓐ $(192 \times 3) - 4$

   Ⓑ $(192 \div 3) - 4$

   Ⓒ $4 - (192 \times 3)$

   Ⓓ $4 - (192 \div 3)$

2   The volume of a single layer in a rectangular prism is 24 cubic centimeters. There are 4 layers in the rectangular prism. What is the volume, in cubic centimeters, of this rectangular prism?

   Ⓐ   6

   Ⓑ   20

   Ⓒ   28

   Ⓓ   96

3   Which expression represents the situation below?

       the number of $\frac{1}{4}$-cup peanut cups that can be filled by 6 cups of peanuts

   Ⓐ $\frac{1}{4} + 6$

   Ⓑ $\frac{1}{4} \times 6$

   Ⓒ $6 - \frac{1}{4}$

   Ⓓ $6 \div \frac{1}{4}$

4   What decimal is equivalent to $\frac{87}{100}$?

    Ⓐ   0.87

    Ⓑ   8.70

    Ⓒ   87.100

    Ⓓ   100.87

5   Which expression could be represented by the shaded parts of the model below?

    Ⓐ $\frac{3}{4} + \frac{1}{5}$

    Ⓑ $\frac{3}{4} \times \frac{1}{5}$

    Ⓒ $\frac{3}{4} + 5$

    Ⓓ $\frac{3}{4} \times 5$

6   Leon drew a polygon in which exactly one angle was a right angle. What kind of polygon could he have drawn?

    Ⓐ   trapezoid

    Ⓑ   rhombus

    Ⓒ   square

    Ⓓ   rectangle

7   Helen makes 120 fluid ounces of lemonade. She sells the lemonade for $2 per cup. How much will Helen make if she sells all the lemonade?

   Ⓐ $10

   Ⓑ $15

   Ⓒ $20

   Ⓓ $30

8   Zachary builds a cube from 1-cm unit cubes and then removes some unit cubes from the front of the cube, as shown below.

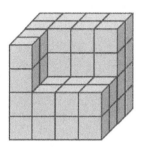

What is the volume of the figure remaining?

   Ⓐ   52 cubic centimeters

   Ⓑ   55 cubic centimeters

   Ⓒ   58 cubic centimeters

   Ⓓ   64 cubic centimeters

9   How many $\frac{1}{4}$-cup servings are in 5 cups?

   Ⓐ $\frac{1}{20}$

   Ⓑ $1\frac{1}{4}$

   Ⓒ   9

   Ⓓ   20

10   Wyatt made the grid below to show the locations of his home, w, and the locations of his friends.

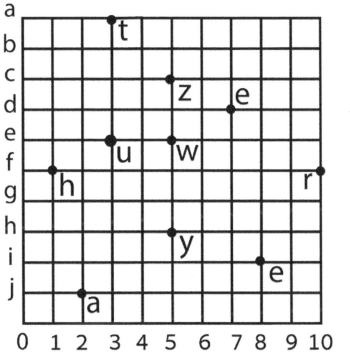

Which friend could Wyatt visit by travelling directly south without making any turns?

Ⓐ   Zoe, represented by z

Ⓑ   Hank, represented by h

Ⓒ   Ursula, represented by u

Ⓓ   Yvonne, represented by y

END OF PRACTICE SET

Mathematics

Grade 5

Practice Set 3

Instructions

Read each question carefully. For each multiple-choice question, fill in the circle for the correct answer. For other types of questions, follow the directions given in the question.

This test should take 45 minutes to complete.

1   Tim plotted four points on the coordinate grid below. Which point would be 5 units from the origin and on the *x*-axis?

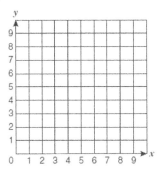

ⒶＡ   (0, 0)

ⒷＢ   (0, 5)

ⒸＣ   (5, 0)

ⒹＤ   (5, 5)

2   The grid below represents the calculation of 0.4 × 0.2.

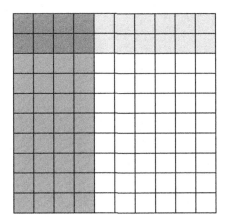

What is the value of 0.4 × 0.2? Write your answer below.

_____

3   Jonah filled the box below with 1-inch cubes. How many 1-inch cubes would it take to fill the box?

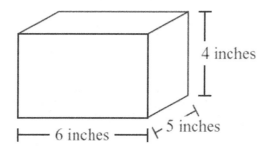

   Ⓐ   15

   Ⓑ   30

   Ⓒ   60

   Ⓓ   120

4   Which ordered pair represents a point located on the line?

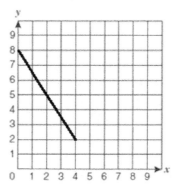

   Ⓐ   (8, 0)

   Ⓑ   (4, 2)

   Ⓒ   (3, 3)

   Ⓓ   (5, 2)

5   Place the sign <, >, or = in each empty box to correctly compare each pair of decimals.

0.06 ☐ 0.006

1.22 ☐ 1.42

5.669 ☐ 5.667

7.535 ☐ 7.505

0.85 ☐ 0.850

9.077 ☐ 9.770

6   Don spends $12.80 on four sandwiches. If each sandwich has the same cost, what is the cost of each sandwich? Write your answer below.

_____

7   A pattern has the rule *y* = 2*x*. A second pattern has the rule *y* = 2*x* + 2. Complete the tables below to find the value of *y* for each value of *x* for the two patterns. Then plot both lines on the coordinate grid.

y = 2*x*

x	y
0	
1	
2	
3	

y = 2*x* + 2

x	y
0	
1	
2	
3	

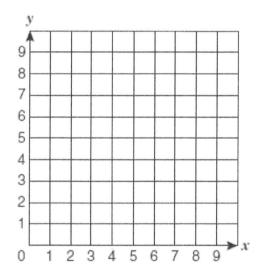

On the lines below, compare the lines on the coordinate grid.

_____

_____

_____

_____

8   A timber shelf has the measurements shown below.

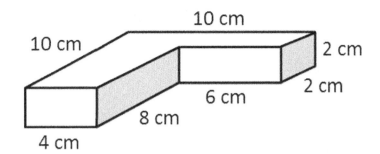

Determine **two** ways the shelf can be divided into two rectangular prisms. Write the dimensions of the **two** sets of rectangular prisms below.

Set 1 _____ by _____ by _____

and

_____ by _____ by _____

Set 2 _____ by _____ by _____

and

_____ by _____ by _____

What is the total volume of the timber shelf? Write your answer below. Be sure to include the correct units.

_____

9   Bradley has 64 1-inch cubic blocks. He uses all the blocks to build a rectangular prism that is 2 inches high and 2 inches wide. How long is the rectangular prism? Write your answer below.

_____ inches

Complete the table below to show the dimensions of **two** other rectangular prisms Bradley could make using all the blocks.

	Rectangular Prism 1	Rectangular Prism 2
Length		
Height		
Width		

Could Bradley use all the blocks to make a cube? Explain your answer.

_____

_____

_____

_____

10   Place the shapes listed below in the correct section of the Venn diagram.

rhombus   rectangle   square

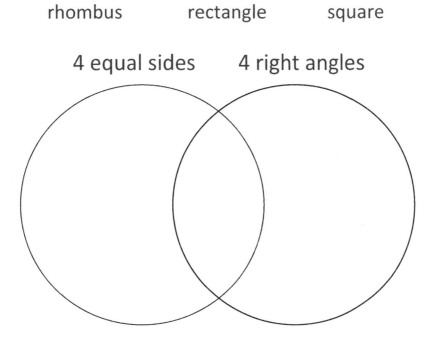

4 equal sides   4 right angles

END OF PRACTICE SET

Mathematics

Grade 5

Practice Set 4

Instructions

Read each question carefully. For each multiple-choice question, fill in the circle for the correct answer. For other types of questions, follow the directions given in the question.

This test should take 45 minutes to complete.

1   Jezebel plots the point (3, 5) on a coordinate grid. Which of these describes where the point would be plotted?

Ⓐ   3 units up from the origin and 5 units left of the *y*-axis

Ⓑ   3 units up from the origin and 5 units right of the *y*-axis

Ⓒ   3 units to the left of the origin and 5 units up from the *x*-axis

Ⓓ   3 units to the right of the origin and 5 units up from the *x*-axis

2   The table shows the best times for running 100 meters of four students on the track team.

Student	Best Time (seconds)
Ramon	12.77
Ellis	12.63
Xavier	12.75
Colin	12.68

If each time is rounded to the nearest tenth, which student would have a best time of 12.7 seconds?

Ⓐ   Ramon

Ⓑ   Ellis

Ⓒ   Xavier

Ⓓ   Colin

3   Annabelle has 56 1-centimeter cubes. What are the dimensions of a rectangular prism Annabelle could build with all the cubes?

    Ⓐ   7 units long, 4 units high, 2 units wide

    Ⓑ   6 units long, 5 units high, 5 units wide

    Ⓒ   10 units long, 2 units high, 3 units wide

    Ⓓ   8 units long, 2 units high, 4 units wide

4   Circle the calculation that is represented on the grid below. Then find the value of the calculation. Write your answer on the line below.

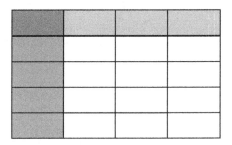

    0.25 ÷ 0.2   0.25 ÷ 4   0.2 ÷ 4   0.2 ÷ 5

    Answer _____

5   Select **all** the expressions below that are equal to $\frac{2}{3}$.

☐ $\frac{1}{3} \times \frac{1}{3}$

☐ $\frac{1}{6} + \frac{1}{6}$

☐ $\frac{1}{3} + \frac{1}{3}$

☐ $\frac{1}{6} \times \frac{1}{6}$

☐ $3 - \frac{1}{3}$

☐ $\frac{5}{12} + \frac{3}{12}$

6   Bryant was reading a book with 220 pages. He read 90 pages in the first week. He wants to finish the book in 5 days. Write an expression that can be used to calculate how many pages he needs to read each day to finish the book in 5 days. Then simplify the expression to find the number of pages he needs to read each day.

Expression _____

Answer _____

7   A factory can fill 225 bottles of orange juice each hour. Each bottle of juice contains 24 fluid ounces of juice. Each bottle of juice sells for $5.50.

How many bottles of juice can be filled in each 12-hour shift? Write your answer below.

_____

If all the bottles made in a 12-hour shift sell, how much money will be made? Write your answer below.

_____

How many fluid ounces of juice are filled in each 12-hour shift? Write your answer below.

_____ fluid ounces

How many pints of juice are filled in each 12-hour shift? Write your answer below.

_____ pints

8   The graph below shows data a science class collected on the diameter of hailstones that fell during a storm.

Hailstone Diameter (inches)

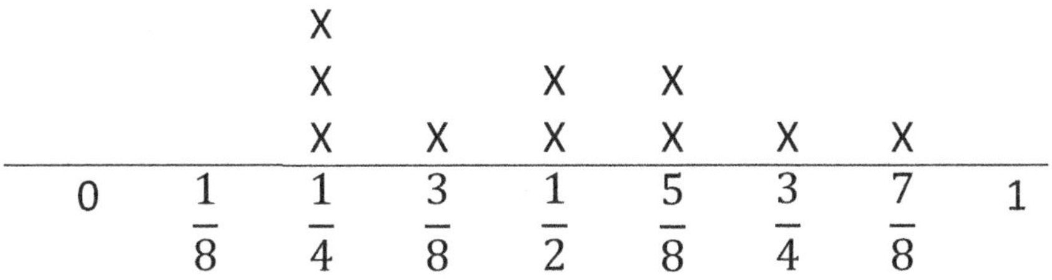

How many hailstones had diameters of $\frac{1}{2}$ inch or more?

Ⓐ   2

Ⓑ   4

Ⓒ   6

Ⓓ   10

9   A pattern has the rule $y = 3x + 1$. Complete the table below to find the value of y for each value of x.

x	y
0	
1	
2	
3	

Plot the points from the table on the coordinate grid below and draw the line that connects the points.

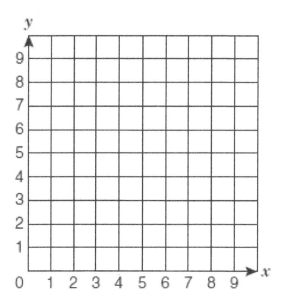

10   Write the names of the shapes below in the correct section of the Venn diagram.

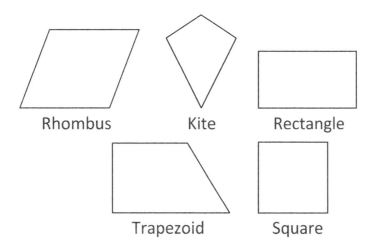

Rhombus   Kite   Rectangle

Trapezoid   Square

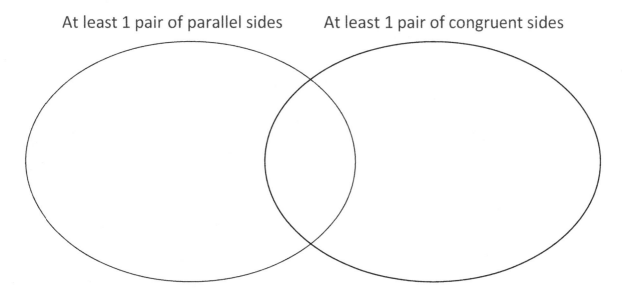

At least 1 pair of parallel sides   At least 1 pair of congruent sides

END OF PRACTICE SET

Mathematics

Grade 5

Practice Set 5

Instructions
Read each question carefully. For each multiple-choice question, fill in the circle for the correct answer. For other types of questions, follow the directions given in the question. This test should take 60 minutes to complete.

1   The table below shows the ticket prices for a bus tour.

Ticket	Price
Adult	$5
Child	$3
Senior	$4

Sam's family paid exactly $15 for bus tickets. Which set of tickets could they have bought?

Ⓐ   1 adult, 2 child, and 1 senior

Ⓑ   2 adult, 1 child

Ⓒ   1 adult, 1 child, 2 senior

Ⓓ   3 child, 1 senior

2   Amanda plotted the four points below on a coordinate grid.

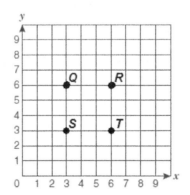

Amanda plots a fifth point that is an equal distance from two of the points. Which of these could be the coordinates of the fifth point?

Ⓐ   (5, 8)

Ⓑ   (3.5, 5)

Ⓒ   (7, 7)

Ⓓ   (9, 4.5)

3   A bakery sold 0.25 of its apple pies by lunch time. What fraction of the apple pies were sold by lunch time?

Ⓐ $\frac{1}{25}$

Ⓑ $\frac{1}{4}$

Ⓒ $\frac{2}{5}$

Ⓓ $\frac{3}{4}$

4   Lisa filled the box below with 1-centimeter cubes. How many 1-centimeter cubes would it take to fill the box?

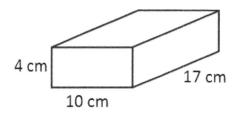

4 cm   17 cm
          10 cm

Ⓐ   160

Ⓑ   556

Ⓒ   680

Ⓓ   1,020

5   Jed has 12 dimes, 18 nickels, and 42 pennies. What is the greatest common factor Jed can use to divide the coins into equal piles? Circle the correct answer.

 2   3   4   6   8   12

6   Erin is sorting 65 quarters into piles. She puts the quarters in piles of 5.

Complete the number sentence below to show how many piles of quarters Erin has.

_____ ÷ _____ = _____

7   Joanne had three singing lessons one week. Two lessons went for 45 minutes, and one lesson went for 60 minutes. Which number sentence could be used to find how many minutes Joanne had singing lessons for?

Ⓐ   (2 x 45) x 60

Ⓑ   (2 + 45) x 60

Ⓒ   (2 x 45) + 60

Ⓓ   (2 + 45) + 60

8   A school has 7 school buses. Each bus can seat 48 students. A total of 303 students get on the buses to go to a school camp. How many empty seats would there be on the buses? Write your answer below.

_____

9   What is the value of the expression below? Write your answer below.

$$(16 + 20) - 8 \div 4$$

_____

10   A jug of milk contains 3 quarts of milk. Michael pours 1 pint of milk from the jug. How many pints of milk are left in the jug? Write your answer below.

_____ pints

11   A talent contest will go for 100 minutes. The contest is divided into 16 equal segments. How long will each segment go for? Write your answer below as a fraction in lowest form.

You can use the hundreds grid below to help you find your answer.

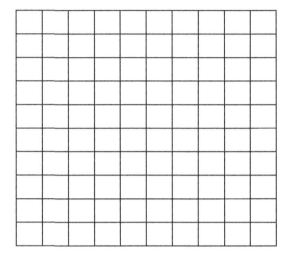

_____ minutes

12   Mike went on vacation to Ohio. When he left home, the odometer read 7,219.4 miles. When he returned home, the odometer read 8,192.6 miles. How many miles did Mike travel? Write your answer below.

_____ miles

13   The table below shows the prices of items at a cake stall.

Item	Price
Small cake	$1.85
Muffin	$2.25
Cookie	$0.95

Frankie bought a small cake and a cookie. Bronwyn bought a muffin. How much more did Frankie spend than Bronwyn? Write your answer below.

_____

14   The grid below represents Dani's living room.

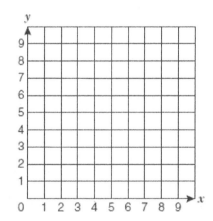

The television is located at the point (5, 4). A lamp is sitting 4 units to the right of the television and 3 units down from the television. What ordered pair represents the location of the lamp? Write your answer below.

_____

15   The diagram shows the length of two pieces of ribbon.

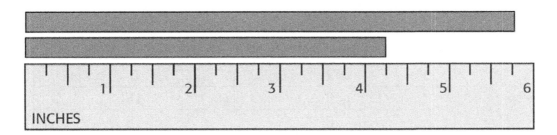

What is the difference in length between the two pieces of ribbon?

Ⓐ $\frac{3}{4}$ inches

Ⓑ $1\frac{1}{4}$ inches

Ⓒ $1\frac{1}{2}$ inches

Ⓓ $1\frac{3}{4}$ inches

16   The table below shows the total cost of hiring DVDs for different numbers of DVDs.

Number of DVDs (*d*)	Total Cost, in Dollars (*C*)
2	6
5	15
6	18
8	24

Write an equation that describes the relationship between the number of DVDs hired, *d*, and the total cost in dollars, *C*. Write your equation below.

_____

17   Which of the following shapes is a parallelogram?

Ⓐ

Ⓑ

Ⓒ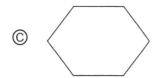

Ⓓ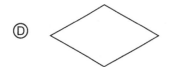

18   At the start of the week, a plant had a height of $\frac{5}{8}$ inches. The plant grew $\frac{1}{4}$ of an inch during the week. Which diagram is shaded to show the height of the plant at the end of the week?

Ⓐ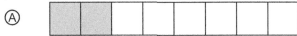

Ⓑ

Ⓒ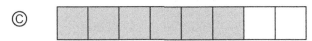

Ⓓ

19   On May 1, Felipe paid $3.58 per gallon of fuel. On August 1, Felipe paid $3.71 per gallon of fuel. By how much did the price of fuel increase?

Ⓐ $0.03

Ⓑ $0.07

Ⓒ $0.13

Ⓓ $0.17

20   Which operation in the expression should be carried out first?

$$6 + 3 \times (8 - 2 \times 2)$$

Ⓐ $6 + 3$

Ⓑ 3×8

Ⓒ $8 - 2$

Ⓓ 2×2

END OF PRACTICE SET

Mathematics

Grade 5

Practice Set 6

Instructions

Read each question carefully. For each multiple-choice question, fill in the circle for the correct answer. For other types of questions, follow the directions given in the question.

This test should take 60 minutes to complete.

1   Shade the diagrams below to show the subtraction. Then write the correct answer below on the blank line.

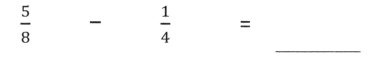

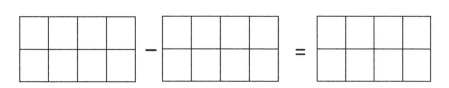

2   Kayla studied for a total of 150 minutes. She spent 50 minutes studying Spanish. What fraction of her total study time did she spend studying Spanish?

Ⓐ $\dfrac{1}{5}$

Ⓑ $\dfrac{1}{4}$

Ⓒ $\dfrac{1}{3}$

Ⓓ $\dfrac{1}{2}$

3   Which of the following measurements is the smallest?

   Ⓐ   1 fluid ounce

   Ⓑ   1 gallon

   Ⓒ   1 pint

   Ⓓ   1 quart

4   Which diagram represents the sum of $\frac{1}{4}$ and $\frac{1}{8}$?

   Ⓐ

   Ⓑ

   Ⓒ

   Ⓓ

5   Which number is less than 35.052?

   Ⓐ   35.009

   Ⓑ   35.061

   Ⓒ   35.101

   Ⓓ   35.077

6   The table below shows a set of number pairs.

x	y
1	2
3	5
5	9

If the points were plotted on a coordinate grid, which of the following would be the coordinates of one of the points?

Ⓐ   (0, 0)

Ⓑ   (2, 1)

Ⓒ   (3, 5)

Ⓓ   (4, 6)

7   A pattern of numbers is shown below.

8, 13, 18, 23, 28, 33, 38, …

Circle **all** the numbers that could be numbers in the pattern.

41   53   60   65   67

71   76   88   92   99

8   An orchard has a total of 192 orange trees. They are planted in rows of 12 orange trees each. How many rows of orange trees does the orchard have? Write your answer below.

_____ rows

9   Joshua bought a pair of sunglasses for $14.85 and a phone case for $2.55. How much change should he receive from $20? Write your answer below.

$ _____

10   The model below was made with 1-inch cubes.

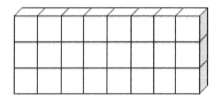

What is the volume of the model? Write your answer below. Be sure to include the correct units in your answer.

_____

11   The graph below shows a line segment. Complete the table below to show the coordinates of three points the line passes through.

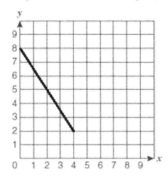

x	0	2	4
y			

What are the coordinates of the point where the line intercepts the *y*-axis? Write your answer below.

_____

12   Candice has a painting canvas that is $\frac{3}{4}$ foot long and $\frac{3}{4}$ foot wide. What is the area of the canvas? Shade the diagram below to find the area of the canvas. Write your answer below.

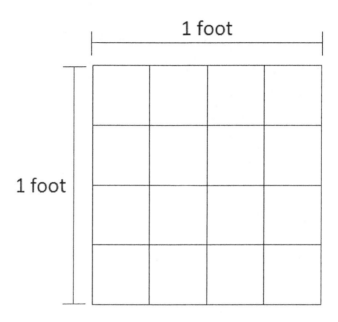

Area: _____ square feet

13 Jasper made a flag for his football team. He painted $\frac{1}{2}$ of the flag blue and $\frac{1}{2}$ of the flag yellow. He added stars to $\frac{1}{3}$ of the blue section. What fraction of the total flag is the blue section with stars? Write your answer below.

_____

14 Shade the model below to show $1\frac{2}{5}$.

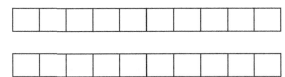

Use the model to find the value of $1\frac{2}{5} \div 2$. Write your answer below.

_____

On the lines below, explain how you found your answer.

_____

_____

_____

_____

_____

15   What are the two smallest 3-digit numbers that can be made using the digits 5, 7, and 2? Each digit must be used only once in each number. Write the two numbers below.

_____ and _____

On the lines below, explain how you found your answer.

_____

_____

_____

_____

_____

16   How is the numeral 55.12 written in words?

Ⓐ   Fifty-five hundred and twelve

Ⓑ   Fifty-five and twelve thousandths

Ⓒ   Fifty-five and twelve hundredths

Ⓓ   Fifty-five and twelve

17 It took James and his family $2\frac{1}{4}$ hours to drive from their house to the beach. How many minutes did the drive take? Write your answer below.

_____ minutes

18 A cat weighs 9 pounds. How many ounces does the cat weigh?

Ⓐ   36 oz

Ⓑ   108 oz

Ⓒ   144 oz

Ⓓ   72 oz

19 What is the value of 10^3?

Ⓐ   30

Ⓑ   100

Ⓒ   1,000

Ⓓ   3,000

20 Which pairs of numbers could be added to the table below? Select **all** the correct answers.

Number	Number ÷ 10
85.04	8.504
501.62	50.162
19.483	1.9483

☐

28.63	286.3

☐

3.65	0.365

☐

987.78	9.8778

☐

62.69	0.6269

☐

7.25	72.5

☐

46.77	4.677

END OF PRACTICE SET

Mathematics

Grade 5

Practice Set 7

Instructions

Read each question carefully. For each multiple-choice question, fill in the circle for the correct answer. For other types of questions, follow the directions given in the question.

This test should take 60 minutes to complete.

1   To add the fractions below, Wayne first needs to determine the least common multiple of the denominators.

$$\frac{1}{5}, \frac{5}{7}, \frac{9}{10}$$

What is the least common multiple of the denominators? Write your answer below.

_____

2   The diagram below shows the length of a piece of ribbon.

$$\frac{12}{100} \text{ meter}$$

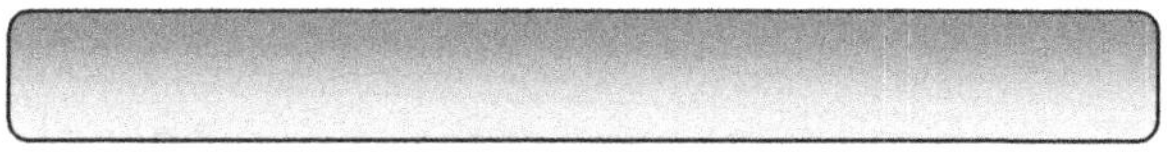

Victoria divides the ribbon into 4 equal pieces. What is the length of each piece of ribbon?

Ⓐ $\frac{2}{25}$ meter

Ⓑ $\frac{3}{25}$ meter

Ⓒ $\frac{12}{25}$ meter

Ⓓ $\frac{3}{100}$ meter

3   Donna has $8.45. She spends $3.75. How much money does Donna have left? Write your answer below.

$_____

4   Hannah cut out a piece of fabric to use for an art project. The length of the fabric was 9.5 yards. The width of the fabric was 3.6 yards less than the length. What was the width of the fabric?

Ⓐ   5.9 yards

Ⓑ   6.9 yards

Ⓒ   12.1 yards

Ⓓ   13.1 yards

5   Errol is putting photos into albums. Each album has 24 pages for holding photos, and each page can hold 8 photographs. How many photographs could Errol put into 3 photo albums?

Ⓐ   192

Ⓑ   376

Ⓒ   486

Ⓓ   576

6   Kathy answered $\frac{3}{5}$ of the questions on a test correctly. Which of the following is equivalent to $\frac{3}{5}$?

    Ⓐ   0.3

    Ⓑ   0.35

    Ⓒ   0.6

    Ⓓ   0.65

7   Which ordered pairs represent a point where the edges of the two rectangles intersect? Select **all** the correct answers.

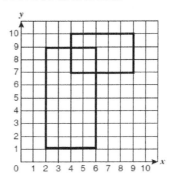

    ☐   (8, 6)

    ☐   (6, 7)

    ☐   (5, 8)

    ☐   (4, 10)

    ☐   (7, 9)

    ☐   (4, 9)

8   To complete a calculation correctly, Mark moves the decimal place of 420.598 two places to the left.

$$420.598 \rightarrow 4.20598$$

Which of these describes the calculation completed?

Ⓐ   Dividing by 10

Ⓑ   Dividing by 100

Ⓒ   Multiplying by 10

Ⓓ   Multiplying by 100

9   Camille cooked a cake on high for $1\frac{1}{4}$ hours. She then cooked it for another $\frac{1}{2}$ hour on low. How long did she cook the cake for in all?

Ⓐ $1\frac{1}{2}$ hours

Ⓑ $1\frac{3}{4}$ hours

Ⓒ $2\frac{1}{4}$ hours

Ⓓ $2\frac{1}{2}$ hours

10   A play sold $224 worth of tickets. Each ticket cost the same amount. Which of these could be the cost of each ticket? Select **all** the possible answers.

☐ $6

☐ $8

☐ $12

☐ $14

☐ $16

☐ $18

11   A piece of note paper has side lengths of 12.5 centimeters. What is the area of the piece of note paper?

Ⓐ   144.25 square centimeters

Ⓑ   144.5 square centimeters

Ⓒ   156.25 square centimeters

Ⓓ   156.5 square centimeters

12   Cody drew a quadrilateral on a coordinate grid, as shown below.

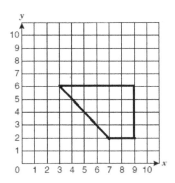

What are the coordinates of the vertices of the quadrilateral? Write the coordinates below.

(___, ___)   (___, ___)   (___, ___)   (___, ___)

13   Sandy has $12.90. Marvin has $18.50. What is the total value of their money? Write your answer below.

$ _____

14   The top of a desk is 4 feet long and 3 feet wide. Raymond wants to cover the top of the desk with a vinyl sheet. The vinyl sheet is measured in square inches. What is the area of the vinyl sheet that will cover the top of the desk exactly?

Ⓐ   12 square inches

Ⓑ   144 square inches

Ⓒ   168 square inches

Ⓓ   1,728 square inches

15   A block is in the shape of a cube. If the side length is represented by *x*, which of these could be used to find the volume of the cube?

Ⓐ $3x$

Ⓑ $6(x^2)$

Ⓒ $6x$

Ⓓ x^3

16   Which sum is represented by the diagram below?

Ⓐ $\dfrac{1}{6} + \dfrac{1}{6}$

Ⓑ $\dfrac{2}{6} + \dfrac{2}{6}$

Ⓒ $\dfrac{3}{6} + \dfrac{3}{6}$

Ⓓ $\dfrac{4}{6} + \dfrac{4}{6}$

17   The point below is translated 2 units to the left and 3 units down. What are the coordinates of the point after the translation?

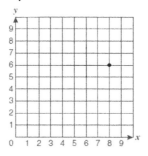

Ⓐ   (6, 3)

Ⓑ   (6, 9)

Ⓒ   (10, 3)

Ⓓ   (10, 9)

18   The table below shows the total number of pounds of flour in different numbers of bags of flour.

Number of Bags	Number of Pounds
3	12
5	20
8	32
9	36

Based on the relationship in the table, how much flour is in each bag? Give your answer in pounds and then ounces. Write your answers below.

_____ pounds

_____ ounces

19   The model below is made up of 1-centimeter cubes. Complete the number sentence below to find the volume of the model.

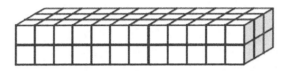

$$\boxed{} \times \boxed{} \times \boxed{} = \boxed{} \ \text{cm}^3$$

20   Which decimal is plotted on the number line below?

Ⓐ   2.25

Ⓑ   2.3

Ⓒ   2.6

Ⓓ   2.75

END OF PRACTICE SET

Mathematics

Grade 5

Practice Set 8

Instructions

Read each question carefully. For each multiple-choice question, fill in the circle for the correct answer. For other types of questions, follow the directions given in the question.

This test should take 60 minutes to complete.

1   Brian made 16 paper cranes in 15 minutes. If he continues making cranes at this rate, how many cranes would he make in 2 hours? Write your answer below.

_____ paper cranes

2   Which word best describes the shape of the sign below?

Ⓐ   Scalene

Ⓑ   Equilateral

Ⓒ   Isosceles

Ⓓ   Right

3   Jason used cubes to make the model shown below. What is the volume of the model?

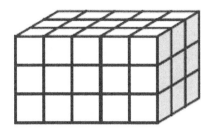

   Ⓐ   15 cubic units

   Ⓑ   45 cubic units

   Ⓒ   50 cubic units

   Ⓓ   75 cubic units

4   The pattern below starts at 0 and uses the rule "Add 4."

0, 4, 8, 12, 16

A second pattern starts at 2 and uses the rule "Add 4." How does the fifth term in the second pattern compare to the fifth term in the first pattern?

   Ⓐ   It is 2 greater.

   Ⓑ   It is 4 greater.

   Ⓒ   It is 8 greater.

   Ⓓ   It is 10 greater.

5   The table below shows a set of number pairs.

x	y
2	−2
3	0
4	2

If the points were plotted on a coordinate grid, which of the following would be the coordinates of one of the points?

Ⓐ   (0, 2)

Ⓑ   (2, 2)

Ⓒ   (4, 2)

Ⓓ   (3, 4)

6   The model below is made up of 1-centimeter cubes. Select the **two** correct ways to find the volume of the cube, in cubic centimeters.

☐   3 + 3 + 3

☐ 3^2

☐ 3^3

☐ $6(3^2)$

☐   3 × 3

☐   3 × 3 × 3

7   Jason is buying baseball cards. Each packet of baseball cards contains 12 baseball cards and costs $3. How many baseball cards can Jason buy for $15? Write your answer below.

_____ baseball cards

8   Which point represents the location of the ordered pair $(1\frac{1}{4}, 2\frac{1}{2})$?

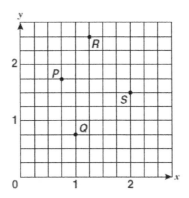

Ⓐ   Point *P*

Ⓑ   Point *Q*

Ⓒ   Point *R*

Ⓓ   Point *S*

9 Which terms describes all the shapes shown below? Select **all** the correct answers.

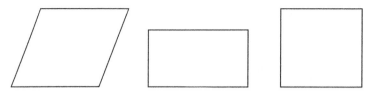

☐ Parallelogram

☐ Rectangle

☐ Rhombus

☐ Quadrilateral

☐ Square

10 The table shows the total cost of hiring different numbers of DVDs.

Number of DVDs	Total Cost, in Dollars
2	6
5	15
6	18
8	24

Which equation could be used to find the total cost in dollars, c, of hiring x DVDs?

Ⓐ $c = x + 4$

Ⓑ $c = 3x$

Ⓒ $c = x + 3$

Ⓓ $c = 8x$

11   Dave bought 4 packets of pies. Three packets had 12 pies each, and one packet had 10 pies. Which number sentence shows the total number of pies Dave bought?

Ⓐ   (3 x 12) x 10

Ⓑ   (3 + 12) x 10

Ⓒ   (3 x 12) + 10

Ⓓ   (3 + 12) + 10

12   Circle each measurement that is the same as 3 yards.

6 feet   9 feet   12 feet   18 feet

36 inches   48 inches   108 inches   144 inches

13   The table below shows the cost of hiring items from a hire store.

Item	Cost per Week
CD	$2
DVD	$3
Video game	$4

Which expression represents the total cost, in dollars, of hiring c CDs and d DVDs for w weeks?

Ⓐ $2c + 3d + w$

Ⓑ $w(2c + 3d)$

Ⓒ $w(2c) + 3d$

Ⓓ $2c + 3d$

14   If the numbers below were each rounded to the nearest tenth, which **two** numbers would be rounded down? Select the **two** correct answers.

☐   17.386

☐   23.758

☐   35.682

☐   54.107

☐   63.453

☐   76.935

15   The model below was made with 1-unit cubes.

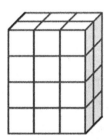

What is the volume of the model? Write your answer below.

_____ cubic units

16   The graph below shows a line segment with three points marked.
Complete the table below to show the coordinates of the three points.

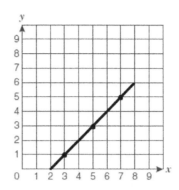

x			
y			

17   Joanne had three singing lessons one week. Two lessons went for 45 minutes, and one lesson went for 60 minutes. Which number sentence could be used to find how many minutes Joanne had singing lessons for?

Ⓐ   2 x (45 + 60)

Ⓑ   (45 + 60) ÷ 3

Ⓒ   (2 x 45) + 60

Ⓓ   (2 × 45) + (2 × 60)

18   How is the numeral 9.007 written in words?

Ⓐ   Nine and seven tenths

Ⓑ   Nine and seven thousandths

Ⓒ   Nine and seven hundredths

Ⓓ   Nine thousand and seven

19   The model below shows $1\frac{6}{100}$ shaded.

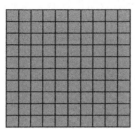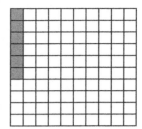

What decimal represents the shaded part of the model? Write your answer below.

_____

20   A rectangular toy box has a length of 90 centimeters, a width of 30 centimeters, and a height of 50 centimeters. What is the volume of the toy box?

Ⓐ   4,500 cubic centimeters

Ⓑ   6,000 cubic centimeters

Ⓒ   81,000 cubic centimeters

Ⓓ   135,000 cubic centimeters

END OF PRACTICE SET

Mathematics

Grade 5

Practice Set 9

Instructions

Read each question carefully. For each multiple-choice question, fill in the circle for the correct answer. For other types of questions, follow the directions given in the question.

This test should take 60 minutes to complete.

1   A glass of water had a temperature of 25°C. Derek heated the water so that the temperature increased by 3°C every 10 minutes. What would the temperature of the water have been after 30 minutes?

     Ⓐ   28°C

     Ⓑ   31°C

     Ⓒ   34°C

     Ⓓ   37°C

2   Mr. Singh bought 2 adult zoo tickets for a total of $22, as well as 4 children's tickets. He spent $54 in total. How much was each children's ticket? Write your answer below.

     $ _____

3   Emily cooked a roast on high for $1\frac{1}{2}$ hours. She then cooked it for another $1\frac{3}{4}$ hour on low. How long did she cook the roast for in all?

     Ⓐ $2\frac{1}{4}$ hours

     Ⓑ $2\frac{3}{4}$ hours

     Ⓒ $3\frac{1}{4}$ hours

     Ⓓ $3\frac{3}{4}$ hours

4   Which operation in the expression should be carried out first?

$$42 + 24 \div (3 - 1) + 5$$

Ⓐ   42 + 24

Ⓑ   24 ÷ 3

Ⓒ   3 − 1

Ⓓ   3 + 5

5   Leanne added $\frac{1}{4}$ cup of milk and $\frac{3}{8}$ cup of water to a bowl. Shade the diagram below to show how many cups of milk and water were in the bowl in all.

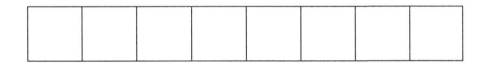

6   A bulldog weighs 768 ounces. How many pounds does the bulldog weigh?

Ⓐ   48 pounds

Ⓑ   64 pounds

Ⓒ   96 pounds

Ⓓ   192 pounds

7   The cost of renting a trailer is a basic fee of $20 plus an additional $25 for each day that the trailer is rented.

Which equation can be used to find *c*, the cost in dollars of the rental for *d* days?

Ⓐ $c = 20d + 25$

Ⓑ $c = 25d + 20$

Ⓒ $c = 20(d + 25)$

Ⓓ $c = 25(d + 20)$

8   Maxwell bought a packet of 48 baseball cards. He gave 8 baseball cards to each of 4 friends. Which number sentence can be used to find the number of baseball cards Maxwell has left?

Ⓐ $(48 - 8) \times 4$

Ⓑ $(48 - 8) \div 4$

Ⓒ $48 - (8 + 4)$

Ⓓ $48 - (8 \times 4)$

9   A square garden has side lengths of $4\frac{1}{2}$ feet. What is the area of the garden? You can use the diagram below to help find the answer.

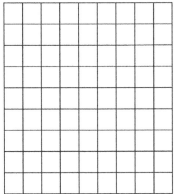

Each square is $\frac{1}{2}$ foot × $\frac{1}{2}$ foot.

Each square has an area of $\frac{1}{4}$ square feet.

Ⓐ $16\frac{1}{4}$ square feet

Ⓑ $20\frac{1}{4}$ square feet

Ⓒ $40\frac{1}{2}$ square feet

Ⓓ $182\frac{1}{4}$ square feet

10   Which two shapes have the same number of sides?

Ⓐ   Triangle and rectangle

Ⓑ   Rectangle and square

Ⓒ   Hexagon and pentagon

Ⓓ   Pentagon and triangle

11   Bryant was reading a book with 220 pages. He read 90 pages in the first week. He wants to finish the book in 5 days. Which expression can be used to calculate how many pages he needs to read each day to finish the book in 5 days?

Ⓐ $220 \div 5 - 90$

Ⓑ $220 - 90 \div 5$

Ⓒ $220 - (90 \div 5)$

Ⓓ $(220 - 90) \div 5$

12   The width of a football field is 160 feet. What is the width of the football field in yards? Write your answer below.

_____ yards

13   Harris and Jamie both started with no savings. Harris saved $3 per week, while Jamie saved $6 per week.

Complete the table below to show Harris's and Jamie's total savings at the end of each week for the first 6 weeks.

Week	1	2	3	4	5	6
Harris's Total Savings						
Jamie's Total Savings						

Describe the relationship between Harris's total savings and Jamie's total savings each week.

_____

_____

_____

_____

_____

14   Which of these is the same as the shaded fraction below?

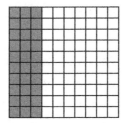

Ⓐ $\dfrac{1}{3} + \dfrac{1}{3} + \dfrac{1}{3}$

Ⓑ $\dfrac{1}{10} + \dfrac{1}{10} + \dfrac{1}{10}$

Ⓒ $\dfrac{1}{30} + \dfrac{1}{30} + \dfrac{1}{30}$

Ⓓ $\dfrac{3}{100} + \dfrac{3}{100} + \dfrac{3}{100}$

15   Tom worked for 32 hours and earned $448. He earned the same rate per hour.

Write an equation that can be solved to find how much Tom earns per hour. Use *h* to represent how much Tom earns per hour.

Equation _____

Solve the equation to find how much Tom earns per hour. Write your answer below.

$ _____

16   Mitch ran 2.6 miles on Monday and 1.8 miles on Tuesday. How many miles less did Mitch run on Tuesday? Write your answer below. You can use the diagram below to find the answer.

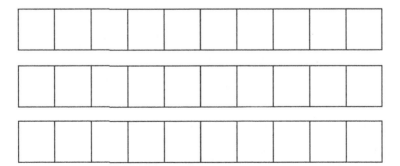

_____ miles

17 The model below is made up of 1-centimeter cubes. What is the volume of the model? Write your answer below.

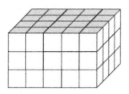

_____ cubic centimeters

18 Joe made the graph below to show the locations of prizes he hid for a treasure hunt. Each star represents a treasure.

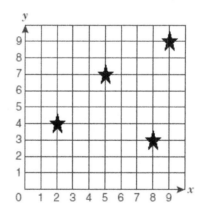

Which ordered pair represents the treasure located closest to the origin? Write your answer below.

_____

19   Sushi sells for $3 for each small roll and $5 for each large roll.

Derrick bought 4 small rolls and 7 large rolls.

Complete the expression below to show how to find the total amount
Derrick spent, in dollars.

$$(\underline{\quad} \times \underline{\quad}) + (\underline{\quad} \times \underline{\quad})$$

Simplify the expression you wrote to find the total amount Derrick spent.
Write your answer below.

$\underline{\hspace{3cm}}$

20   There are 200 students at Kerry's elementary school. Of those students, $\frac{2}{5}$
are fifth grade students. How many fifth grade students are there? Write
your answer below.

$\underline{\hspace{4cm}}$ students

END OF PRACTICE SET

Mathematics

Grade 5

Practice Set 10

Instructions
Read each question carefully. For each multiple-choice question, fill in the circle for the correct answer. For other types of questions, follow the directions given in the question. This test should take 60 minutes to complete.

1   The decimal cards for 0.59 and 0.22 are shown below.

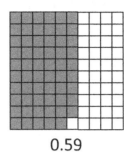

0.59   0.22

What is the difference of 0.59 and 0.22? Write your answer below.

_____

2   Look at the fractions below.

$$1\frac{1}{3},\ 2\frac{1}{2},\ 3\frac{5}{6}$$

Which procedure can be used to find the sum of the fractions?

Ⓐ   Find the sum of the whole numbers, find the sum of the fractions, and then add the two sums

Ⓑ   Find the sum of the whole numbers, find the sum of the fractions, and then multiply the two sums

Ⓒ   Find the sum of the whole numbers, find the sum of the fractions, and then subtract the two sums

Ⓓ   Find the sum of the whole numbers, find the sum of the fractions, and then divide the two sums

3   Joy made 24 apple pies for a bake sale. Each serving was $\frac{1}{8}$ of a pie. How many servings did Joy make?

    Ⓐ   3

    Ⓑ   32

    Ⓒ   96

    Ⓓ   192

4   The graph shows the line segment *ST*. Point *S* is at (2, 5). Point *T* is at (9, 5).

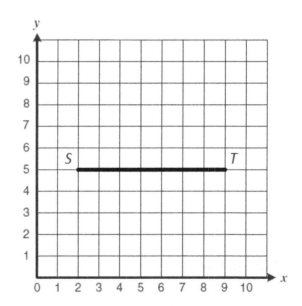

Which of these shows how to find the length of the line segment?

    Ⓐ   5 + 5

    Ⓑ   9 – 5

    Ⓒ   9 – 2

    Ⓓ   2 + 9

5   A diner has 18 tables. Each table can seat 4 people. The diner also has 8 benches that can each seat 6 people. How many people can the diner seat in all?

    Ⓐ   36

    Ⓑ   120

    Ⓒ   260

    Ⓓ   308

6   A fraction representing $\frac{6}{8}$ is shown below.

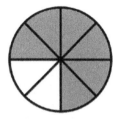

What is the value of $\frac{6}{8} \div 3$?

    Ⓐ $\frac{1}{8}$

    Ⓑ $\frac{3}{8}$

    Ⓒ $\frac{1}{4}$

    Ⓓ $\frac{3}{4}$

7   What is the value of the expression below? Write your answer below.

$$42 + 24 \div 3 + 3$$

_____

8   Keegan's family drinks about 2 gallons of milk every 5 days.

About how much milk does Keegan's family drink in 30 days? Give your answer in gallons, quarts, and pints. Write your answers below.

_____ gallons

_____ quarts

_____ pints

9 Chan spent $\frac{3}{8}$ of his total homework time completing his science homework. What calculation could be used to convert the fraction to a decimal?

Ⓐ $3 \div 8 \times 100$

Ⓑ $8 \div 3 \times 100$

Ⓒ $3 \div 8$

Ⓓ $8 \div 3$

10 A recipe for pancakes requires $2\frac{2}{3}$ cups of flour. Donna only has $1\frac{1}{2}$ cups of flour. How many more cups of flour does Donna need?

Ⓐ $\frac{1}{3}$ cup

Ⓑ $\frac{1}{6}$ cup

Ⓒ $1\frac{1}{3}$ cups

Ⓓ $1\frac{1}{6}$ cups

11 There are 6 reams of paper in a box. There are 144 boxes of paper on a pallet. How many reams of paper are on a pallet? Write your answer below.

_____

12 Byron made 9 baskets out of 15 baskets he attempted. What fraction of his baskets did he make? Write the fraction below and then simplify it to lowest terms.

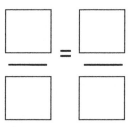

13 The mass of a car is 1.56 tons. What is the mass of the car in pounds?

Ⓐ   312 pounds

Ⓑ   3,120 pounds

Ⓒ   31,200 pounds

Ⓓ   312,000 pounds

14 The table below shows a set of number pairs.

x	y
1	1
3	5
5	9

Which equation shows the relationship between x and y?

Ⓐ $y = x + 2$

Ⓑ $y = x + 4$

Ⓒ $y = 2x - 1$

Ⓓ $y = 3x - 4$

15   Leonard bought 12 tickets to a charity event. The total cost of the tickets was $216. The expression below can be used to find the cost of each ticket.

$$216 \div 12$$

Which of the following is equivalent to the above expression?

Ⓐ   (240 ÷ 12) + (24 ÷ 12)

Ⓑ   (200 ÷ 10) + (16 ÷ 2)

Ⓒ   (216 ÷ 10) + (216 ÷ 2)

Ⓓ   (120 ÷ 12) + (96 ÷ 12)

16   Which terms describe the figure below? Select **all** the correct answers.

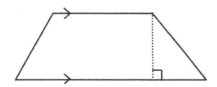

☐   Parallelogram

☐   Polygon

☐   Quadrilateral

☐   Trapezoid

17   Write the coordinates of the points shown on the grid below. Write your answers below.

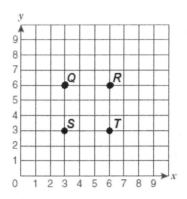

Point *Q*   (___ , ___)   Point *R*   (___ , ___)

Point *S*   (___ , ___)   Point *T*   (___ , ___)

18   The table below shows the relationship between the original price and the sale price of a book.

Original price, P	Sale price, S
$10	$7.50
$12	$9
$14	$10.50
$16	$12

What is the rule to find the sale price of a book, in dollars? Add the missing number to the rule below.

$$S = \text{\_\_\_\_} \; P$$

19 Leo measures the length, width, and height of a block. He multiplies the length, width, and height. What is Leo finding?

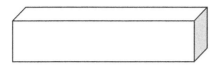

Ⓐ   Surface area

Ⓑ   Mass

Ⓒ   Volume

Ⓓ   Perimeter

20 Circle **all** the figures below that do NOT have any parallel sides.

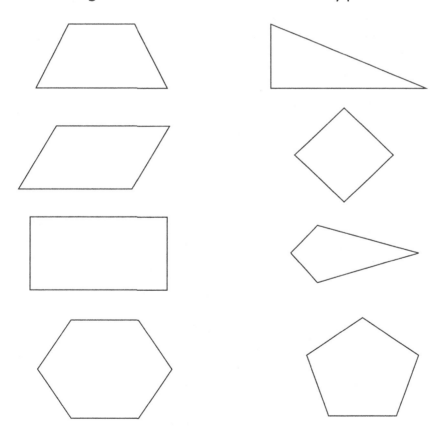

END OF PRACTICE SET

Mathematics

Grade 5

Practice Set 11

Instructions

Read each question carefully. For each multiple-choice question, fill in the circle for the correct answer. For other types of questions, follow the directions given in the question.

This test should take 60 minutes to complete.

1   The cost of renting a windsurfer is a basic fee of $15 plus an additional $5 for each hour that the windsurfer is rented. Which equation can be used to find c, the cost in dollars of the rental for h hours?

Ⓐ $c = 15h + 5$

Ⓑ $c = 5h + 15$

Ⓒ $c = 15(h + 5)$

Ⓓ $c = 5(h + 15)$

2   The graph below shows the line segment PQ. Point P is at (3, 9). Point Q is at (3, 1).

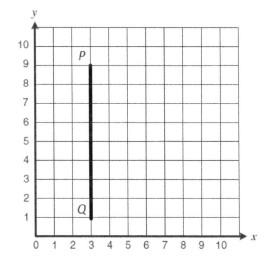

What is the length of the line segment PQ? Write your answer below.

_____ units

3   What decimal is equivalent to the fraction $\frac{33}{100}$?

    Ⓐ   0.033

    Ⓑ   0.33

    Ⓒ   33.0

    Ⓓ   3.3

4   Which decimal is represented below?

$$(4 \times 100) + (8 \times 1) + (6 \times \frac{1}{100}) + (3 \times \frac{1}{1000})$$

    Ⓐ   480.63

    Ⓑ   480.063

    Ⓒ   408.63

    Ⓓ   408.063

5   If $p = 5$, what is the value of $4(p + 7)$? Write your answer below.

_____

6   In the number 787,421 how much greater is the value represented by the 7 in the hundred thousands place than the value represented by the 7 in the thousands place?

Ⓐ   1

Ⓑ   10

Ⓒ   100

Ⓓ   1,000

7   The table below shows the total number of lemons in different numbers of bags of lemons.

Number of Bags (B)	Number of Lemons (L)
2	16
3	24
5	40
8	64

What is the relationship between the total number of lemons, L, and the number of bags of lemons, B? Complete the equation below to show the relationship.

$$L = \text{\_\_\_} B$$

8   Amy ordered 3 pizzas for $6.95 each. She also bought a soft drink for $1.95. Which equation can be used to find how much change, c, she should receive from $30?

    Ⓐ $c = 30 - 3(6.95 + 1.95)$

    Ⓑ $c = 30 - 3(6.95 - 1.95)$

    Ⓒ $c = 30 - 6.95 - 1.95$

    Ⓓ $c = 30 - (6.95 \times 3) - 1.95$

9   What is the decimal 55.146 rounded to the nearest whole number, nearest tenth, and nearest hundredth? Write your answers below.

Nearest whole number _____

Nearest tenth _____

Nearest hundredth _____

10   What is the value of the expression below? Write your answer below.

$$28 + 4 \div 2 + (9 - 5)$$

_____

11   The table shows the side length of a rhombus and the perimeter of a rhombus.

Side Length, x (cm)	Perimeter, y (cm)
1	4
2	8
3	12
4	16

Which equation represents the relationship between side length and perimeter?

Ⓐ $y = x + 3$

Ⓑ $y = 4x$

Ⓒ $x = y + 4$

Ⓓ $x = 4y$

12   A florist sells balloons in sets of 6. A customer ordered several sets of 6 balloons. Which of these could be the total number of balloons ordered? Circle **all** the correct possible answers.

48   50   54   58   62

66   70   78   80   88

13   The table shows the amount of Don's phone bill for four different months.

Month	Amount
April	$12.22
May	$12.09
June	$12.18
July	$12.05

Place the months in order from the lowest bill to the highest bill. Write the months on the lines below.

Lowest   _____

           _____

           _____

Highest   _____

14   Marcus sold drinks at a lemonade stand. The table shows how many drinks of each size he sold.

Size	Number Sold
Small	15
Medium	20
Large	5
Extra large	10

Which size drink made up $\frac{3}{10}$ of the total sold? Write your answer below.

_____

15   What is the rule to find the value of a term in the sequence below?

Position, n	Value of Term
1	3
2	5
3	7
4	9

Ⓐ $4n - 4$

Ⓑ $3n$

Ⓒ $2n + 1$

Ⓓ $n + 2$

16   The table shows the amount of rainfall for the first five days of May.

Date	1st	2nd	3rd	4th	5th
Rainfall (cm)	4.59	4.18	4.50	4.61	4.73

Compare the five decimals. Write the decimals on the lines below.

_____ < _____ < _____ < _____ < _____

17   What value of *x* makes the equation below true? Write your answer below.

$$54 \div x = 9$$

x = _____

18   The grid below represents 4 x 7.

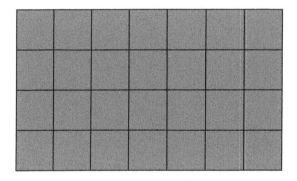

Which of these is another way to represent 4 x 7? Select **all** the correct answers.

☐ 7×4

☐ $7 + 7 + 7 + 7$

☐ $7 + 7 + 7 + 7 + 7 + 7 + 7$

☐ $4 + 4 + 4 + 4$

☐ $4 \times 4 \times 4 \times 4$

☐ $4 + 4 + 4 + 4 + 4 + 4 + 4$

19   Sandy has 129 dimes. Marvin has 185 dimes. What is the total value of Sandy and Marvin's dimes?

    Ⓐ $3.04

    Ⓑ $3.14

    Ⓒ $30.40

    Ⓓ $31.40

20   Which of the following is a correct definition of a square?

    Ⓐ   A rectangle with two pairs of parallel sides

    Ⓑ   A rectangle with adjacent sides perpendicular

    Ⓒ   A rhombus with four equal sides

    Ⓓ   A rhombus with four right angles

END OF PRACTICE SET

Mathematics

Grade 5

Practice Set 12

Instructions

Read each question carefully. For each multiple-choice question, fill in the circle for the correct answer. For other types of questions, follow the directions given in the question.

This test should take 60 minutes to complete.

1   Ellen multiplies the number 3 by a fraction. The result is a number greater than 3. Which of these could be the fraction?

Ⓐ $1\frac{1}{4}$

Ⓑ $\frac{8}{9}$

Ⓒ $\frac{1}{6}$

Ⓓ $\frac{1}{2}$

2   Look at the two sequences of numbers below.

First sequence: 0, 4, 8, 12, 16, 20, 24, ...
Second sequence: 0, 8, 16, 24, 32, 40, 48, ...

If the 100th term in the first sequence is represented as n, which of these gives the 100th term in the second sequence?

Ⓐ $n + 4$

Ⓑ $n + 8$

Ⓒ $2n$

Ⓓ $2n + 4$

3   Lloyd bought 4 T-shirts. Each T-shirt cost $7. Which is one way to work out how much change Lloyd would receive from $30?

Ⓐ   Add 4 to 7 and subtract the result from 30

Ⓑ   Add 4 to 7 and add the result to 30

Ⓒ   Multiply 4 by 7 and add the result to 30

Ⓓ   Multiply 4 by 7 and subtract the result from 30

4   An Italian restaurant sells four types of meals. The owner made this table to show how many meals of each type were sold one night. According to the table, which statements are true? Select **all** the correct statements.

Meal	Number Sold
Pasta	16
Pizza	18
Salad	11
Risotto	9

☐   The store sold more pizza meals than salad and risotto meals combined.

☐   The store sold twice as many pizza meals as risotto meals.

☐   The store sold more pasta meals than any other type of meal.

☐   The store sold half as many salad meals as pasta meals.

☐   The store sold over 50 meals in total.

5   Jordan is putting CDs in a case. She can fit 24 CDs in each row. She has 120 CDs. Which equation can be used to find the total number of rows, *r*, she can fill?

Ⓐ $r \times 120 = 24$

Ⓑ $r \div 24 = 120$

Ⓒ $120 \times 24 = r$

Ⓓ $120 \div 24 = r$

6   Jay made 8 trays of 6 muffins each.

He gave 12 muffins away. He packed the remaining muffins in bags of 4 muffins each. Which expression can be used to find how many bags of muffins he packed?

Ⓐ $(8 \times 6) - 12 \div 4$

Ⓑ $(8 \times 6) - (12 \div 4)$

Ⓒ $8 \times (6 - 12 \div 4)$

Ⓓ $(8 \times 6 - 12) \div 4$

7   The table shows the side length of an equilateral triangle and the perimeter of an equilateral triangle.

Side Length, *l* (inches)	Perimeter, *P* (inches)
2	6
3	9
4	12
5	15

Which equation represents the relationship between side length and perimeter?

Ⓐ $P = l + 4$

Ⓑ $P = 3l$

Ⓒ $l = P + 4$

Ⓓ $l = 3P$

8   Grade 5 students held a vote on where to go for a field trip. The results are shown below.

Location	Number of Votes
Museum	|||| |||| ||
Cinema	|||| |||| ||||	
Zoo	|||| |||| |||| ||||
Town Hall	|||| ||||

Chen decides to make a picture graph to show the results. He wants to use the ☺ symbol to represent 4 votes. How many ☺ symbols should be placed in the column for "Zoo?" Write your answer below.

_____ symbols

9   Complete the missing numbers to write 600,000 in three more different ways.

6,000   hundreds

_____ thousands

_____ ten-thousands

_____ hundred-thousands

10   Which statement is true about the product of $\frac{1}{3}$ and 6?

Ⓐ   The product is greater than 6.

Ⓑ   The product is less than $\frac{1}{3}$.

Ⓒ   The product is a value between the two factors.

Ⓓ   The product is a value equal to one of the factors.

11 Which number makes the number sentence below true?

$$2 \div \square = 8$$

Ⓐ $\frac{1}{2}$

Ⓑ $\frac{1}{4}$

Ⓒ $\frac{1}{8}$

Ⓓ $\frac{1}{16}$

12 Lewis scored $\frac{3}{20}$ of the points in a basketball game. How many of the team's 120 points did Lewis score?

Ⓐ 15

Ⓑ 18

Ⓒ 20

Ⓓ 35

13   The grid below represents Roberto's backyard.

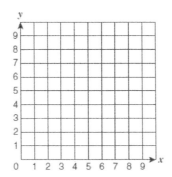

A lemon tree is located at the point (6, 5). An orange tree is located 2 units to the right and 3 units up from the lemon tree. Find the coordinates that represent the location of the orange tree. Write the coordinates below.

_____

Explain how you found your answer.

_____

_____

_____

_____

14   Look at the figure below.

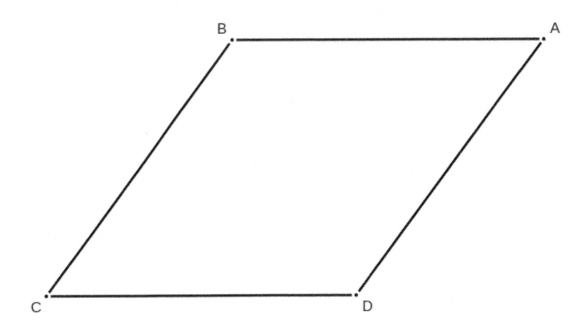

Identify the two pairs of parallel line segments. Write each line segment on one of the lines below.

_____ and _____, _____ and _____

Name the shape and describe the properties you used to identify it.

_____

_____

_____

_____

15   The statements below describe quadrilaterals.

         At least 1 pair of parallel sides

         2 pairs of perpendicular sides

         4 equal angles

         4 right angles

         4 congruent sides

Circle the statement that correctly describes a trapezoid.

Which statement above could be used to tell the difference between a rectangle and a square? Explain your answer.

_____

_____

_____

_____

_____

16   A restaurant manager kept a record of the pieces of pie sold one week. He made this list to show the results.

- $\frac{1}{4}$ of the pieces sold were apple pie
- $\frac{3}{8}$ of the pieces sold were pumpkin pie
- $\frac{1}{12}$ of the pieces sold were cherry pie
- The rest of the pieces sold were peach pie.

What fraction of the pieces sold were peach pie? Write your answer below.

_____

If there were a total of 360 pieces of pie sold that week, how many pieces of cherry pie were sold? Write your answer below.

_____

17   Karen made this table to show the amount she spent on lunch each day one week.

Day	Amount
Monday	$5.73
Tuesday	$5.49
Wednesday	$5.51
Thursday	$5.27
Friday	$5.80

What is the total amount Karen spent on lunch that week? Write your answer below.

$ _____

18   Plot the number 3.8 on the number line below.

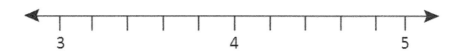

What is 3.8 rounded to the nearest whole number? Write your answer below.

_____

On the lines below, explain how the number line helped you round the number.

_____

_____

_____

19   Circle the measurements that are equivalent to 600 centimeters.

0.6 mm   6 mm   60 mm   6000 mm

0.6 m   6 m   60 m   6000 m

Convert 600 centimeters to kilometers. Write your answer below.

_____ kilometers

20   The model below is made up of 1-centimeter cubes.

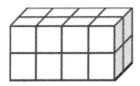

Write and solve an equation to find the volume of the model.

Volume: _____ cubic centimeters

If the height of the model is doubled, how does the volume of the model change? Explain your answer.

_____

_____

_____

_____

END OF PRACTICE SET

ANSWER KEY

About Ohio's Mathematics Standards

Student learning in Ohio is based on the skills described in Ohio's Learning Standards. In 2017, Ohio's Learning Standards for Mathematics were revised. Beginning in the 2018-2019 school year, the state tests will assess these revised standards. Just like the real state tests, the questions in this book assess whether students have the knowledge and skills described in the revised standards.

Assessing Skills and Knowledge

The skills listed in Ohio's Learning Standards are divided into five topics, or clusters. These are:

- Operations and Algebraic Thinking
- Number and Operations in Base Ten
- Number and Operations – Fractions
- Measurement and Data
- Geometry

The answer key identifies the topic for each question. Use the topics listed to identify general areas of strength and weakness. Then target revision and instruction accordingly.

The answer key also identifies the specific math skill that each question is testing. Use the skills listed to identify skills that the student is lacking. Then target revision and instruction accordingly.

Scoring Questions

This book includes questions where a task needs to be completed or a written answer is provided. The answer key gives guidance on what to look for in the answer and how to score these questions. Use the criteria listed as a guide to scoring these questions, and as a guide for giving the student advice on how to improve an answer.

Mathematics, Practice Set 1

Question	Answer	Topic	Mathematics Standard
1	D	Number & Operations in Base Ten	Find whole number quotients of whole numbers with up to four-digit dividends and two-digit divisors, using strategies based on place value, the properties of operations, and/or the relationship between multiplication and division. Illustrate and explain the calculation by using equations, rectangular arrays, and/or area models.
2	B	Number & Operations-Fractions	Add and subtract fractions with unlike denominators (including mixed numbers and fractions greater than 1) by replacing given fractions with equivalent fractions in such a way as to produce an equivalent sum or difference of fractions with like denominators.
3	A	Number & Operations in Base Ten	Fluently multiply multi-digit whole numbers using a standard algorithm.
4	A	Measurement & Data	Display and interpret data in graphs (picture graphs, bar graphs, and line plots) to solve problems using numbers and operations for this grade.
5	D	Number & Operations-Fractions	Use benchmark fractions and number sense of fractions to estimate mentally and assess the reasonableness of answers.
6	D	Number & Operations in Base Ten	Fluently multiply multi-digit whole numbers using a standard algorithm.
7	B	Geometry	Identify and describe commonalities and differences between types of quadrilaterals based on angle measures, side lengths, and the presence or absence of parallel and perpendicular lines.
8	B	Number & Operations-Fractions	Explain why multiplying a given number by a fraction less than 1 results in a product smaller than the given number.
9	A	Geometry	Identify and describe commonalities and differences between types of triangles based on angle measures (equiangular, right, acute, and obtuse triangles) and side lengths (isosceles, equilateral, and scalene triangles).
10	C	Measurement & Data	Convert between pounds and ounces; miles and feet; yards, feet, and inches; gallons, quarts, pints, cups, and fluid ounces; hours, minutes, and seconds in solving multi-step, real-world problems.

Mathematics, Practice Set 2

Question	Answer	Topic	Mathematics Standard
1	B	Operations/Algebraic Thinking	Write simple expressions that record calculations with numbers, and interpret numerical expressions without evaluating them.
2	D	Measurement & Data	Find the volume of a right rectangular prism with whole number side lengths by packing it with unit cubes, and show that the volume is the same as would be found by multiplying the edge lengths.
3	D	Number & Operations-Fractions	Solve real-world problems involving division of unit fractions by non-zero whole numbers and division of whole numbers by unit fractions.
4	A	Number & Operations-Fractions	Interpret a fraction as division of the numerator by the denominator.
5	D	Number & Operations-Fractions	Apply and extend previous understandings of multiplication to multiply a fraction or whole number by a fraction.
6	A	Geometry	Identify and describe commonalities and differences between types of quadrilaterals based on angle measures, side lengths, and the presence or absence of parallel and perpendicular lines.
7	D	Measurement & Data	Convert between pounds and ounces; miles and feet; yards, feet, and inches; gallons, quarts, pints, cups, and fluid ounces; hours, minutes, and seconds in solving multi-step, real-world problems.
8	A	Measurement & Data	Recognize volume as additive. Find volumes of solid figures composed of two non-overlapping right rectangular prisms by adding the volumes of the non-overlapping parts, applying this technique to solve real-world problems.
9	D	Number & Operations-Fractions	Solve real-world problems involving division of unit fractions by non-zero whole numbers and division of whole numbers by unit fractions.
10	D	Geometry	Represent real-world and mathematical problems by graphing points in the first quadrant of the coordinate plane, and interpret coordinate values of points in the context of the situation.

Mathematics, Practice Set 3

Question	Answer	Topic	Mathematics Standard
1	C	Geometry	Use a pair of perpendicular number lines, called axes, to define a coordinate system, with the intersection of the lines (the origin) arranged to coincide with the 0 on each line and a given point in the plane located by using an ordered pair of numbers, called its coordinates. Understand that the first number indicates how far to travel from the origin in the direction of one axis, and the second number indicates how far to travel in the direction of the second axis, with the convention that the names of the two axes and the coordinates correspond.
2	0.08	Number & Operations in Base Ten	Perform operations with multi-digit whole numbers and with decimals to hundredths.
3	D	Measurement & Data	Measure volumes by counting unit cubes, using cubic cm, cubic in, cubic ft, and improvised units.
4	B	Geometry	Use a pair of perpendicular number lines, called axes, to define a coordinate system, with the intersection of the lines (the origin) arranged to coincide with the 0 on each line and a given point in the plane located by using an ordered pair of numbers, called its coordinates.
5	>, <, >, >, =, <	Number & Operations in Base Ten	Compare two decimals to thousandths based on meanings of the digits in each place, using >, =, and < symbols to record the results of comparisons.
6	$3.20	Number & Operations in Base Ten	Divide whole numbers by decimals and decimals by whole numbers.
7	See Below	Operations/Algebraic Thinking	Form ordered pairs consisting of corresponding terms from two patterns. Graph the ordered pairs on a coordinate plane.
8	See Below	Measurement & Data	Recognize volume as additive. Find volumes of solid figures composed of two non-overlapping right rectangular prisms by adding the volumes of the non-overlapping parts, applying this technique to solve real-world problems.
9	See Below	Measurement & Data	Find the volume of a right rectangular prism with whole number side lengths by packing it with unit cubes, and show that the volume is the same as would be found by multiplying the edge lengths.
10	See Below	Geometry	Identify and describe commonalities and differences between types of quadrilaterals based on angle measures, side lengths, and the presence or absence of parallel and perpendicular lines.

Q7.
The first table should be completed with the *y* values 0, 2, 4, and 6.
The second table should be completed with the *y* values 2, 4, 6, and 8.
The two lines should be graphed as shown below.

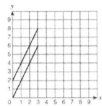

The student should give a reasonable comparison of the lines. The comparison should include that the lines are parallel and that the second line is 2 units above the first line.

Scoring Information
Give a total score out of 6.
Give a score of 1 for each table correctly completed.
Give a score of 1 for each line correctly graphed.
Give a score out of 2 for the comparison of the lines.

Q8.
The following two sets of dimensions should be listed. (Measurements can be listed in any order.)
10 cm by 2 cm by 2 cm and 4 cm by 8 cm by 2 cm
4 cm by 10 cm by 2 cm and 6 cm by 2 cm by 2 cm

Answer: 104 cubic centimeters or 104 cm^3

Scoring Information
Give a total score out of 3.
Give a score of 1 for each set of correct dimensions.
Give a score of 1 for the correct answer.

Q9.
16 inches
Each column in the table should be completed with any combination of length, height, and width that multiply to 64. Possible answers include: 4, 8, and 2; 64, 1, and 1; 8, 8, and 1; or 32, 2, and 1.

The student should identify that Bradley could make a cube. The explanation should describe how the cube would have side lengths of 4 and a volume of 64 cubic inches. The explanation may include the calculation 4 × 4 × 4 = 64.

Scoring Information
Give a total score out of 6.
Give a score of 1 for a correct answer of 16 inches.
Give a score of 1 for each column of the table completed correctly.
Give a score of 1 for identifying that Bradley could make a cube.
Give a score out of 2 for the explanation.

Q10.
Circle for "4 equal sides": rhombus
Circle for "4 right angles": rectangle
Overlapping circles: square

Scoring Information
Give a total score out of 3.
Give a score of 1 for each shape correctly placed.

Mathematics, Practice Set 4

Question	Answer	Topic	Mathematics Standard
1	D	Geometry	Use a pair of perpendicular number lines, called axes, to define a coordinate system, with the intersection of the lines (the origin) arranged to coincide with the 0 on each line and a given point in the plane located by using an ordered pair of numbers, called its coordinates.
2	D	Number & Operations in Base Ten	Compare two decimals to thousandths based on meanings of the digits in each place, using >, =, and < symbols to record the results of comparisons.
3	A	Measurement & Data	Find the volume of a right rectangular prism with whole number side lengths by packing it with unit cubes, and show that the volume is the same as would be found by multiplying the edge lengths.
4	0.2 ÷ 4 0.05	Number & Operations in Base Ten	Divide whole numbers by decimals and decimals by whole numbers.
5	3rd, 5th, and 6th	Number & Operations-Fractions	Use benchmark fractions and number sense of fractions to estimate mentally and assess the reasonableness of answers.
6	(220 – 90) ÷ 5 26	Operations/Algebraic Thinking	Use parentheses in numerical expressions, and evaluate expressions with this symbol.
7	See Below	Number & Operations in Base Ten	Perform operations with multi-digit whole numbers and with decimals to hundredths.
8	C	Measurement & Data	Display and interpret data in graphs (picture graphs, bar graphs, and line plots) to solve problems using numbers and operations for this grade.
9	See Below	Geometry	Represent real-world and mathematical problems by graphing points in the first quadrant of the coordinate plane, and interpret coordinate values of points in the context of the situation.
10	See Below	Geometry	Identify and describe commonalities and differences between types of quadrilaterals based on angle measures, side lengths, and the presence or absence of parallel and perpendicular lines.

Q7.
2,700
$14,850
64,800 fluid ounces
4,050 pints

Scoring Information
Give a total score out of 4.
Give a score of 1 for each correct answer.

Q9.
The table should be completed with the *y* values 1, 4, 7, and 10.
The line should be graphed as shown below.

Scoring Information
Give a total score out of 3.
Give a score of 0.5 for each correct value in the table.
Give a score of 1 for the line correctly graphed.

Q10.
Circle for "At least 1 pair of parallel sides": Trapezoid
Circle for "At least 1 pair of congruent sides": Kite
Overlapping circles: Rhombus, Rectangle, Square

Scoring Information
Give a total score out of 5.
Give a score of 1 for each shape correctly placed.

Mathematics, Practice Set 5

Question	Answer	Topic	Mathematics Standard
1	A	Number & Operations in Base Ten	Perform operations with multi-digit whole numbers.
2	D	Geometry	Represent real-world and mathematical problems by graphing points in the first quadrant of the coordinate plane, and interpret coordinate values of points in the context of the situation.
3	B	Number & Operations-Fractions	Interpret a fraction as division of the numerator by the denominator.
4	C	Measurement & Data	Find the volume of a right rectangular prism with whole number side lengths by packing it with unit cubes.
5	6	Number & Operations in Base Ten	Find whole number quotients of whole numbers with up to four-digit dividends and two-digit divisors, using strategies based on place value, the properties of operations, and/or the relationship between multiplication and division. Illustrate and explain the calculation by using equations, rectangular arrays, and/or area models.
6	$65 \div 5 = 13$	Number & Operations in Base Ten	Find whole number quotients of whole numbers with up to four-digit dividends and two-digit divisors, using strategies based on place value, the properties of operations, and/or the relationship between multiplication and division. Illustrate and explain the calculation by using equations, rectangular arrays, and/or area models.
7	C	Operations/Algebraic Thinking	Write simple expressions that record calculations with numbers, and interpret numerical expressions without evaluating them.
8	33	Number & Operations in Base Ten	Fluently multiply multi-digit whole numbers using a standard algorithm.
9	34	Operations/Algebraic Thinking	Use parentheses in numerical expressions, and evaluate expressions with this symbol.
10	5 pints	Measurement & Data	Convert between pounds and ounces; miles and feet; yards, feet, and inches; gallons, quarts, pints, cups, and fluid ounces; hours, minutes, and seconds in solving multi-step, real-world problems.
11	$6\frac{1}{4}$ minutes	Number & Operations-Fractions	Solve word problems involving division of whole numbers leading to answers in the form of fractions or mixed numbers.
12	973.2 miles	Number & Operations in Base Ten	Add and subtract decimals, including decimals with whole numbers.
13	$0.55 or 55 cents	Number & Operations in Base Ten	Add and subtract decimals, including decimals with whole numbers.
14	(9, 1)	Geometry	Represent real-world and mathematical problems by graphing points in the first quadrant of the coordinate plane, and interpret coordinate values of points in the context of the situation.
15	C	Number & Operations-Fractions	Solve word problems involving addition and subtraction of fractions referring to the same whole, including cases of unlike denominators, e.g., by using visual fraction models or equations to represent the problem.

16	$C = 3d$	Operations/Algebraic Thinking	Analyze patterns and relationships by identifying apparent relationships between corresponding terms.
17	D	Geometry	Identify and describe commonalities and differences between types of quadrilaterals based on angle measures, side lengths, and the presence or absence of parallel and perpendicular lines.
18	D	Number & Operations-Fractions	Add and subtract fractions with unlike denominators (including mixed numbers and fractions greater than 1) by replacing given fractions with equivalent fractions in such a way as to produce an equivalent sum or difference of fractions with like denominators.
19	C	Number & Operations in Base Ten	Add and subtract decimals, including decimals with whole numbers.
20	D	Operations/Algebraic Thinking	Use parentheses in numerical expressions, and evaluate expressions with this symbol.

Mathematics, Practice Set 6

Question	Answer	Topic	Mathematics Standard
1	$\frac{3}{8}$	Number & Operations-Fractions	Add and subtract fractions with unlike denominators (including mixed numbers and fractions greater than 1) by replacing given fractions with equivalent fractions in such a way as to produce an equivalent sum or difference of fractions with like denominators.
2	C	Number & Operations-Fractions	Solve word problems involving division of whole numbers leading to answers in the form of fractions.
3	A	Measurement & Data	Know relative sizes of these U.S. customary measurement units: pounds, ounces, miles, yards, feet, inches, gallons, quarts, pints, cups, fluid ounces, hours, minutes, and seconds.
4	B	Number & Operations-Fractions	Add and subtract fractions with unlike denominators (including mixed numbers and fractions greater than 1) by replacing given fractions with equivalent fractions in such a way as to produce an equivalent sum or difference of fractions with like denominators.
5	A	Number & Operations in Base Ten	Compare two decimals to thousandths based on meanings of the digits in each place, using >, =, and < symbols to record the results of comparisons.
6	C	Operations/Algebraic Thinking	Form ordered pairs consisting of corresponding terms from two patterns, and graph the ordered pairs on a coordinate plane.
7	53, 88	Operations/Algebraic Thinking	Analyze patterns and relationships by identifying apparent relationships between corresponding terms.
8	16 rows	Number & Operations in Base Ten	Find whole number quotients of whole numbers with up to four-digit dividends and two-digit divisors, using strategies based on place value, the properties of operations, and/or the relationship between multiplication and division. Illustrate and explain the calculation by using equations, rectangular arrays, and/or area models.
9	$2.60	Number & Operations in Base Ten	Add and subtract decimals, including decimals with whole numbers.
10	24 cubic inches	Measurement & Data	Measure volumes by counting unit cubes, using cubic cm, cubic in, cubic ft, and improvised units.
11	See Below	Geometry	Represent real-world and mathematical problems by graphing points in the first quadrant of the coordinate plane, and interpret coordinate values of points in the context of the situation.
12	See Below	Number & Operations-Fractions	Multiply fractional side lengths to find areas of rectangles, and represent fraction products as rectangular areas.
13	$\frac{1}{6}$	Number & Operations-Fractions	Apply and extend previous understandings of multiplication to multiply a fraction by a fraction.
14	See Below	Number & Operations-Fractions	Interpret division of a unit fraction by a non-zero whole number, and compute such quotients.
15	See Below	Number & Operations in Base Ten	Recognize that in a multi-digit number, a digit in one place represents 10 times as much as it represents in the place to its right and 1/10 of what it represents in the place to its left.
16	C	Number & Operations in Base Ten	Read and write decimals to thousandths using base-ten numerals, number names, and expanded form.

17	135 minutes	Number & Operations-Fractions	Solve real-world problems involving multiplication of fractions and mixed numbers.
18	C	Measurement & Data	Convert between pounds and ounces; miles and feet; yards, feet, and inches; gallons, quarts, pints, cups, and fluid ounces; hours, minutes, and seconds in solving multi-step, real-world problems.
19	C	Number & Operations in Base Ten	Explain patterns in the number of zeros of the product when multiplying a number by powers of 10, and explain patterns in the placement of the decimal point when a decimal is multiplied or divided by a power of 10.
20	3.65, 0.365 46.77, 4.677	Number & Operations in Base Ten	Explain patterns in the number of zeros of the product when multiplying a number by powers of 10, and explain patterns in the placement of the decimal point when a decimal is multiplied or divided by a power of 10.

Q11.
The student should complete the table as shown below.

x	0	2	4
y	8	5	2

Answer: (0, 8)

Scoring Information
Give a total score out of 4.
Give a score of 1 for each correct value added to the table.
Give a score of 1 for the correct answer.

Q12.
The diagram should be shaded to show a 3 × 3 section, as shown. The student should recognize that 9 out of 16 squares are shaded, so the area is $\frac{9}{16}$ square feet.

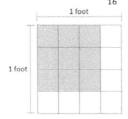

Area: $\frac{9}{16}$ square feet

Scoring Information
Give a total score out of 2.
Give a score of 1 for shading the diagram correctly.
Give a score of 1 for the correct answer.

Q14.

The model should have 14 squares shaded.

Answer: $\frac{7}{10}$

The student should describe using half of the shaded squares to represent $1\frac{2}{5} \div 2$, and seeing on the diagram that this is equal to 7 of the 10 squares. The student could also describe adding half of the whole number 1 to half of the fraction $\frac{2}{5}$.

Scoring Information

Give a total score out of 4.

Give a score of 1 for the correct shading.

Give a score of 1 for the correct answer.

Give a score out of 2 for the explanation.

Q15.

257 and 275

The explanation should refer to the place value of the numbers. It may describe how the number with the lowest value should be in the hundreds place.

Scoring Information

Give a total score out of 4.

Give a score of 1 for each correct number.

Give a score out of 2 for the explanation.

Mathematics, Practice Set 7

Question	Answer	Topic	Mathematics Standard
1	70	Number & Operations-Fractions	Add and subtract fractions with unlike denominators (including mixed numbers and fractions greater than 1) by replacing given fractions with equivalent fractions in such a way as to produce an equivalent sum or difference of fractions with like denominators.
2	D	Number & Operations-Fractions	Solve real-world problems involving division of unit fractions by non-zero whole numbers and division of whole numbers by unit fractions.
3	$4.70	Number & Operations in Base Ten	Add and subtract decimals, including decimals with whole numbers.
4	A	Number & Operations in Base Ten	Add and subtract decimals, including decimals with whole numbers.
5	D	Number & Operations in Base Ten	Fluently multiply multi-digit whole numbers using a standard algorithm.
6	C	Number & Operations-Fractions	Interpret a fraction as division of the numerator by the denominator.
7	(4, 9) (6, 7)	Geometry	Represent real-world and mathematical problems by graphing points in the first quadrant of the coordinate plane, and interpret coordinate values of points in the context of the situation.
8	B	Number & Operations in Base Ten	Explain patterns in the number of zeros of the product when multiplying a number by powers of 10, and explain patterns in the placement of the decimal point when a decimal is multiplied or divided by a power of 10.
9	B	Number & Operations-Fractions	Add and subtract fractions with unlike denominators (including mixed numbers and fractions greater than 1) by replacing given fractions with equivalent fractions in such a way as to produce an equivalent sum or difference of fractions with like denominators.
10	$8, $14, $16	Number & Operations in Base Ten	Find whole number quotients of whole numbers with up to four-digit dividends and two-digit divisors, using strategies based on place value, the properties of operations, and/or the relationship between multiplication and division. Illustrate and explain the calculation by using equations, rectangular arrays, and/or area models.
11	C	Number & Operations in Base Ten	Multiply whole numbers by decimals.
12	(3, 6) (9, 6) (9, 2) (7, 2)	Geometry	Represent real-world and mathematical problems by graphing points in the first quadrant of the coordinate plane, and interpret coordinate values of points in the context of the situation.
13	$31.40	Number & Operations in Base Ten	Add and subtract decimals, including decimals with whole numbers.
14	D	Measurement & Data	Convert between pounds and ounces; miles and feet; yards, feet, and inches; gallons, quarts, pints, cups, and fluid ounces; hours, minutes, and seconds in solving multi-step, real-world problems.
15	D	Measurement & Data	Measure volumes by counting unit cubes, using cubic cm, cubic in, cubic ft, and improvised units.

16	B	Number & Operations-Fractions	Use benchmark fractions and number sense of fractions to estimate mentally and assess the reasonableness of answers.
17	A	Geometry	Represent real-world and mathematical problems by graphing points in the first quadrant of the coordinate plane, and interpret coordinate values of points in the context of the situation.
18	4 pounds 64 ounces	Measurement & Data	Convert between pounds and ounces; miles and feet; yards, feet, and inches; gallons, quarts, pints, cups, and fluid ounces; hours, minutes, and seconds in solving multi-step, real-world problems.
19	$2 \times 3 \times 12 = 72$ cm^3	Measurement & Data	Relate volume to the operations of multiplication and addition.
20	C	Number & Operations in Base Ten	Read and write decimals to thousandths using base-ten numerals, number names, and expanded form.

Mathematics, Practice Set 8

Question	Answer	Topic	Mathematics Standard
1	128	Measurement & Data	Convert between pounds and ounces; miles and feet; yards, feet, and inches; gallons, quarts, pints, cups, and fluid ounces; hours, minutes, and seconds in solving multi-step, real-world problems.
2	B	Geometry	Identify and describe commonalities and differences between types of triangles based on angle measures (equiangular, right, acute, and obtuse triangles) and side lengths (isosceles, equilateral, and scalene triangles).
3	B	Measurement & Data	Measure volumes by counting unit cubes, using cubic cm, cubic in, cubic ft, and improvised units.
4	A	Operations/Algebraic Thinking	Generate two numerical patterns using two given rules. Identify apparent relationships between corresponding terms.
5	C	Operations/Algebraic Thinking	Form ordered pairs consisting of corresponding terms from the two patterns, and graph the ordered pairs on a coordinate plane.
6	3^3 $3 \times 3 \times 3$	Measurement & Data	Relate volume to the operations of multiplication and addition.
7	60 baseball cards	Number & Operations in Base Ten	Perform operations with multi-digit whole numbers.
8	C	Geometry	Represent real-world and mathematical problems by graphing points in the first quadrant of the coordinate plane, and interpret coordinate values of points in the context of the situation.
9	Parallelogram Quadrilateral	Geometry	Identify and describe commonalities and differences between types of quadrilaterals based on angle measures, side lengths, and the presence or absence of parallel and perpendicular lines.
10	B	Operations/Algebraic Thinking	Analyze patterns and relationships by identifying apparent relationships between corresponding terms.
11	C	Operations/Algebraic Thinking	Write simple expressions that record calculations with numbers, and interpret numerical expressions without evaluating them.
12	9 feet 108 inches	Measurement & Data	Convert between pounds and ounces; miles and feet; yards, feet, and inches; gallons, quarts, pints, cups, and fluid ounces; hours, minutes, and seconds in solving multi-step, real-world problems.
13	B	Operations/Algebraic Thinking	Use parentheses in numerical expressions, and evaluate expressions with this symbol.
14	35.682 63.543	Number & Operations in Base Ten	Use place value understanding to round decimals to any place, millions through hundredths.
15	24 cubic units	Measurement & Data	Measure volumes by counting unit cubes, using cubic cm, cubic in, cubic ft, and improvised units.
16	x 3 5 7 y 1 3 5	Operations/Algebraic Thinking	Form ordered pairs consisting of corresponding terms from two patterns. Graph the ordered pairs on a coordinate plane.
17	C	Operations/Algebraic Thinking	Write simple expressions that record calculations with numbers, and interpret numerical expressions without evaluating them.
18	B	Number & Operations in Base Ten	Read and write decimals to thousandths using base-ten numerals, number names, and expanded form.

| 19 | 1.06 | Number & Operations in Base Ten | Explain patterns in the number of zeros of the product when multiplying a number by powers of 10, and explain patterns in the placement of the decimal point when a decimal is multiplied or divided by a power of 10. |
| 20 | D | Measurement & Data | Relate volume to the operations of multiplication and addition and solve real-world and mathematical problems involving volume. |

Mathematics, Practice Set 9

Question	Answer	Topic	Mathematics Standard
1	C	Operations/Algebraic Thinking	Analyze patterns and relationships.
2	$8	Number & Operations in Base Ten	Perform operations with multi-digit whole numbers.
3	C	Number & Operations-Fractions	Add and subtract fractions with unlike denominators (including mixed numbers and fractions greater than 1) by replacing given fractions with equivalent fractions in such a way as to produce an equivalent sum or difference of fractions with like denominators.
4	C	Operations/Algebraic Thinking	Use parentheses in numerical expressions, and evaluate expressions with this symbol.
5	5 of the 8 squares shaded	Number & Operations-Fractions	Add and subtract fractions with unlike denominators (including mixed numbers and fractions greater than 1) by replacing given fractions with equivalent fractions in such a way as to produce an equivalent sum or difference of fractions with like denominators.
6	A	Measurement & Data	Convert between pounds and ounces; miles and feet; yards, feet, and inches; gallons, quarts, pints, cups, and fluid ounces; hours, minutes, and seconds in solving multi-step, real-world problems.
7	B	Operations/Algebraic Thinking	Write simple expressions that record calculations with numbers, and interpret numerical expressions without evaluating them.
8	D	Operations/Algebraic Thinking	Write simple expressions that record calculations with numbers, and interpret numerical expressions without evaluating them.
9	B	Number & Operations-Fractions	Find the area of a rectangle with fractional side lengths by tiling it with unit squares of the appropriate unit fraction side lengths, and show that the area is the same as would be found by multiplying the side lengths.
10	B	Geometry	Identify and describe commonalities and differences between types of quadrilaterals based on angle measures, side lengths, and the presence or absence of parallel and perpendicular lines.
11	D	Operations/Algebraic Thinking	Write simple expressions that record calculations with numbers, and interpret numerical expressions without evaluating them.
12	$53\frac{1}{3}$ yards	Measurement & Data	Convert between pounds and ounces; miles and feet; yards, feet, and inches; gallons, quarts, pints, cups, and fluid ounces; hours, minutes, and seconds in solving multi-step, real-world problems.
13	See Below	Operations/Algebraic Thinking	Generate two numerical patterns using two given rules. Identify apparent relationships between corresponding terms.
14	B	Number & Operations-Fractions	Use benchmark fractions and number sense of fractions to estimate mentally and assess the reasonableness of answers.

15	448 = 32*h* $14	Number & Operations in Base Ten	Find whole number quotients of whole numbers with up to four-digit dividends and two-digit divisors, using strategies based on place value, the properties of operations, and/or the relationship between multiplication and division. Illustrate and explain the calculation by using equations, rectangular arrays, and/or area models.
16	0.8 miles	Number & Operations in Base Ten	Add and subtract decimals, including decimals with whole numbers.
17	60 cubic centimeters	Measurement & Data	Measure volumes by counting unit cubes, using cubic cm, cubic in, cubic ft, and improvised units.
18	(2, 4)	Geometry	Represent real-world and mathematical problems by graphing points in the first quadrant of the coordinate plane, and interpret coordinate values of points in the context of the situation.
19	(4 × 3) + (7 × 5) $47	Operations/Algebraic Thinking	Use parentheses in numerical expressions, and evaluate expressions with this symbol.
20	80 students	Number & Operations-Fractions	Apply and extend previous understandings of multiplication to multiply a fraction or whole number by a fraction.

Q13.
The student should complete the table with the following values:

Harris's Total Savings	3	6	9	12	15	18
Jamie's Total Savings	6	12	18	24	30	36

The student should explain that Jamie's total savings are always twice Harris's total savings.

Scoring Information
Give a total score out of 4.
Give a score of 1 for the correct values for Harris's Total Savings.
Give a score of 1 for the correct values for Jamie's Total Savings.
Give a score out of 2 for the explanation.

Mathematics, Practice Set 10

Question	Answer	Topic	Mathematics Standard
1	0.37	Number & Operations in Base Ten	Add and subtract decimals, including decimals with whole numbers.
2	A	Number & Operations-Fractions	Add and subtract fractions with unlike denominators (including mixed numbers and fractions greater than 1) by replacing given fractions with equivalent fractions in such a way as to produce an equivalent sum or difference of fractions with like denominators.
3	D	Number & Operations-Fractions	Solve real-world problems involving division of unit fractions by non-zero whole numbers and division of whole numbers by unit fractions.
4	C	Geometry	Represent real-world and mathematical problems by graphing points in the first quadrant of the coordinate plane, and interpret coordinate values of points in the context of the situation.
5	B	Number & Operations in Base Ten	Fluently multiply multi-digit whole numbers using a standard algorithm.
6	C	Number & Operations-Fractions	Interpret division of a unit fraction by a non-zero whole number, and compute such quotients.
7	53	Operations/Algebraic Thinking	Use parentheses in numerical expressions, and evaluate expressions with this symbol.
8	12 gallons 48 quarts 96 pints	Measurement & Data	Convert between pounds and ounces; miles and feet; yards, feet, and inches; gallons, quarts, pints, cups, and fluid ounces; hours, minutes, and seconds in solving multi-step, real-world problems.
9	C	Number & Operations-Fractions	Interpret a fraction as division of the numerator by the denominator.
10	D	Number & Operations-Fractions	Add and subtract fractions with unlike denominators (including mixed numbers and fractions greater than 1) by replacing given fractions with equivalent fractions in such a way as to produce an equivalent sum or difference of fractions with like denominators.
11	864	Number & Operations in Base Ten	Fluently multiply multi-digit whole numbers using a standard algorithm.
12	9/15 = 3/5	Number & Operations-Fractions	Interpret a fraction as division of the numerator by the denominator.
13	B	Measurement & Data	Convert like measurement units within a given measurement system.
14	C	Operations/Algebraic Thinking	Analyze patterns and relationships by identifying apparent relationships between corresponding terms.
15	D	Number & Operations in Base Ten	Find whole number quotients of whole numbers with up to four-digit dividends and two-digit divisors, using strategies based on place value, the properties of operations, and/or the relationship between multiplication and division. Illustrate and explain the calculation by using equations, rectangular arrays, and/or area models.
16	Polygon Quadrilateral Trapezoid	Geometry	Identify and describe commonalities and differences between types of quadrilaterals based on angle measures, side lengths, and the presence or absence of parallel and perpendicular lines.

17	Point Q (3, 6) Point R (6, 6) Point S (3, 3) Point T (6, 3)	Geometry	Represent real-world and mathematical problems by graphing points in the first quadrant of the coordinate plane, and interpret coordinate values of points in the context of the situation.
18	$S = 0.75p$ OR $S = \frac{3}{4}p$	Operations/Algebraic Thinking	Analyze patterns and relationships by identifying apparent relationships between corresponding terms.
19	C	Measurement & Data	Measure volumes by counting unit cubes, using cubic cm, cubic in, cubic ft, and improvised units.
20	triangle kite pentagon	Geometry	Identify and describe commonalities and differences between types of quadrilaterals based on angle measures, side lengths, and the presence or absence of parallel and perpendicular lines.

Mathematics, Practice Set 11

Question	Answer	Topic	Mathematics Standard
1	B	Operations/Algebraic Thinking	Write simple expressions that record calculations with numbers, and interpret numerical expressions without evaluating them.
2	8 units	Geometry	Represent real-world and mathematical problems by graphing points in the first quadrant of the coordinate plane, and interpret coordinate values of points in the context of the situation.
3	B	Number & Operations in Base Ten	Explain patterns in the number of zeros of the product when multiplying a number by powers of 10, and explain patterns in the placement of the decimal point when a decimal is multiplied or divided by a power of 10.
4	D	Number & Operations in Base Ten	Read and write decimals to thousandths using base-ten numerals, number names, and expanded form.
5	48	Operations/Algebraic Thinking	Use parentheses in numerical expressions, and evaluate expressions with this symbol.
6	C	Number & Operations in Base Ten	Recognize that in a multi-digit number, a digit in one place represents 10 times as much as it represents in the place to its right and 1/10 of what it represents in the place to its left.
7	$L = 8B$	Operations/Algebraic Thinking	Analyze patterns and relationships by identifying apparent relationships between corresponding terms.
8	D	Operations/Algebraic Thinking	Write simple expressions that record calculations with numbers, and interpret numerical expressions without evaluating them.
9	55 55.1 55.15	Number & Operations in Base Ten	Use place value understanding to round decimals to any place, millions through hundredths.
10	34	Operations/Algebraic Thinking	Use parentheses in numerical expressions, and evaluate expressions with this symbol.
11	B	Operations/Algebraic Thinking	Analyze patterns and relationships by identifying apparent relationships between corresponding terms.
12	48 54 66 78	Number & Operations in Base Ten	Find whole number quotients of whole numbers with up to four-digit dividends and two-digit divisors, using strategies based on place value, the properties of operations, and/or the relationship between multiplication and division. Illustrate and explain the calculation by using equations, rectangular arrays, and/or area models.
13	July May June April	Number & Operations in Base Ten	Compare two decimals to thousandths based on meanings of the digits in each place, using >, =, and < symbols to record the results of comparisons.
14	Small	Number & Operations-Fractions	Interpret a fraction as division of the numerator by the denominator. Solve word problems involving division of whole numbers leading to answers in the form of fractions or mixed numbers.
15	C	Operations/Algebraic Thinking	Analyze patterns and relationships by identifying apparent relationships between corresponding terms.
16	4.18 < 4.50 < 4.59 < 4.61 < 4.73	Number & Operations in Base Ten	Compare two decimals to thousandths based on meanings of the digits in each place, using >, =, and < symbols to record the results of comparisons.

17	6	Number & Operations in Base Ten	Find whole number quotients of whole numbers with up to four-digit dividends and two-digit divisors, using strategies based on place value, the properties of operations, and/or the relationship between multiplication and division. Illustrate and explain the calculation by using equations, rectangular arrays, and/or area models.
18	1st, 2nd, and 6th	Number & Operations in Base Ten	Perform operations with multi-digit whole numbers.
19	D	Number & Operations in Base Ten	Explain patterns in the number of zeros of the product when multiplying a number by powers of 10, and explain patterns in the placement of the decimal point when a decimal is multiplied or divided by a power of 10.
20	D	Geometry	Identify and describe commonalities and differences between types of quadrilaterals based on angle measures, side lengths, and the presence or absence of parallel and perpendicular lines.

Mathematics, Practice Set 12

Question	Answer	Topic	Mathematics Standard
1	A	Number & Operations-Fractions	Explain why multiplying a given number by a fraction greater than 1 results in a product greater than the given number.
2	C	Operations/Algebraic Thinking	Generate two numerical patterns using two given rules. Identify apparent relationships between corresponding terms.
3	D	Number & Operations in Base Ten	Perform operations with multi-digit whole numbers.
4	2nd and 5th	Number & Operations in Base Ten	Perform operations with multi-digit whole numbers.
5	D	Number & Operations in Base Ten	Find whole number quotients of whole numbers with up to four-digit dividends and two-digit divisors.
6	D	Operations/Algebraic Thinking	Write simple expressions that record calculations with numbers, and interpret numerical expressions without evaluating them.
7	B	Operations/Algebraic Thinking	Analyze patterns and relationships by identifying apparent relationships between corresponding terms.
8	5 symbols	Measurement & Data	Display and interpret data in graphs (picture graphs, bar graphs, and line plots) to solve problems using numbers and operations for this grade.
9	600 60 6	Number & Operations in Base Ten	Recognize that in a multi-digit number, a digit in one place represents 10 times as much as it represents in the place to its right and 1/10 of what it represents in the place to its left.
10	C	Number & Operations-Fractions	Apply and extend previous understandings of multiplication to multiply a fraction or whole number by a fraction.
11	B	Number & Operations-Fractions	Interpret division of a whole number by a unit fraction, and compute such quotients.
12	B	Number & Operations-Fractions	Apply and extend previous understandings of multiplication to multiply a whole number by a fraction.
13	See Below	Geometry	Represent real-world and mathematical problems by graphing points in the first quadrant of the coordinate plane, and interpret coordinate values of points in the context of the situation.
14	See Below	Geometry	Identify and describe commonalities and differences between types of quadrilaterals based on angle measures, side lengths, and the presence or absence of parallel and perpendicular lines.
15	See Below	Geometry	Identify and describe commonalities and differences between types of quadrilaterals based on angle measures, side lengths, and the presence or absence of parallel and perpendicular lines.
16	$\frac{7}{24}$, 30	Number & Operations-Fractions	Add and subtract fractions. Apply and extend previous understandings of multiplication to multiply a fraction or whole number by a fraction.
17	$27.80	Number & Operations in Base Ten	Add and subtract decimals, including decimals with whole numbers.
18	See Below	Number & Operations in Base Ten	Use place value understanding to round decimals to any place, millions through hundredths.

19	6000 mm, 6 m 0.006 kilometers	Measurement & Data	Convert like measurement units within a given measurement system.
20	See Below	Measurement & Data	Relate volume to the operations of multiplication and addition.

Q13.
(8, 8)

The student may describe the calculation (6 + 2, 5 + 3) = (8, 8), or may describe plotting the new point on the grid and reading the coordinates.

Scoring Information
Give a total score out of 3.
Give a score of 1 for the correct answer.
Give a score out of 2 for the explanation.

Q14.
BA and CD, BC and AD

The student should identify that the shape is a rhombus. The explanation should refer to the two pairs of parallel sides and the four sides being equal in length. The explanation may also include that the shape is not a square because the angles are not right angles.

Scoring Information
Give a total score out of 4.
Give a score of 0.5 for each correct pair listed.
Give a score of 1 for the correct shape identified.
Give a score out of 2 for the explanation.

Q15.
The student should circle the statement below.
At least 1 pair of parallel sides

The student should identify that 4 congruent sides could be used to tell the difference between a rectangle and a square. The answer should show an understanding that all the statements are true for both rectangles and squares except that a square has 4 congruent sides and a rectangle does not.

Scoring Information
Give a total score out of 4.
Give a score of 1 for the correct statement circled.
Give a score of 1 for identifying the correct statement.
Give a score out of 2 for the explanation.

Q18.
The number 3.8 should be plotted on the number line.
Answer: 4
The student should explain how you can tell that the number is closer to 4 than 3.

Scoring Information
Give a total score out of 3.
Give a score of 1 for the number correctly plotted.
Give a score of 1 for the correct answer.
Give a score out of 1 for the explanation.

Q20.
The student should write and solve the equation 2 × 2 × 4 = 16.
Volume: 16 cubic centimeters

The student should identify that the volume would double if the height doubled. The student could explain that doubling one of the values in the calculation doubles the result. The student could also double the height and show that 4 × 2 × 4 = 32, which is double 16.

Scoring Information
Give a total score out of 4.
Give a score of 1 for a correct equation.
Give a score of 1 for the correct volume.
Give a score out of 2 for the explanation.

Made in United States
Orlando, FL
03 April 2023

31674936R00078